# They Came to Paris

*Bookstalls along the Seine*

# They Came to Paris

*by* HOWARD GREENFELD

CROWN PUBLISHERS, INC., NEW YORK

Manufactured in the United States of America
Published simultaneously in Canada by General Publishing Company Limited
First Edition
The text of this book is set in 14 pt. Bodoni
The illustrations are black and white photographs,
reproduced in halftone.

Library of Congress Cataloging in Publication Data

Greenfeld, Howard
    They came to Paris.

    Bibliography: p.
    SUMMARY:  Briefly discusses the artistic and social
climate of Paris during the 1920's and describes the experiences of the many American artists, writers, and
musicians who chose to live and work there.
    1. Paris—Intellectual life—Juvenile literature.
2. Americans in Paris—Juvenile literature. 3. Authors,
American—Biography—Juvenile literature. [1. Americans
in Paris. 2. Paris—Intellectual life. 3. Authors,
American—Biography] I. Title.
DC715.G79    944'.36'00413    75-2413

ISBN  0-517-51848-1

*to* HELENA STRASSOVA

# Contents

# Introduction

"Things must be better elsewhere. . . ."

How many young Americans—above all those with even a glimmer of creative talent—have spoken those words and then packed their bags and left home! They have set out from their small towns in Nebraska or Georgia or Maine to serve their artistic apprenticeships in Chicago, San Francisco, or New York in order to escape what seem to be the suffocating restrictions of their hometowns, as well as a set of values that seem false to them. Often it has been an angry act, one of rebellion. Less angry have been those who have gone off to a university, there to live in a community of their peers, in a society that ideally should encourage them in the pursuit of ideas, which should challenge them to find their own way—in the company of others with similar goals and ambitions.

It is a universal need to do one's own thing, as we put it today; not alone, but preferably in the company of sympathetic, congenial contemporaries.

This desire to get away, to achieve personal independence, is a healthy one. Self-reliance, which is gained from moving out of one's habitual surroundings, encourages originality, especially in the arts. In the United States, a young country with only two centuries of tradition, it has in the past been natural for the discontented young to turn to another continent—to Europe—to benefit from a seemingly wiser civilization, rich in history and experience. Today, however, for the most part, those young Americans who want to carve out their own world have turned less to Europe—the gap between the two continents has narrowed —and more to the major cities of their own country, and even to the rural areas, back to nature in an attempt to get away from what seem to them the false values of the city.

In the past, however, the discontented instinctively turned to the Old World, so much so that expatriation to Europe actually became a tradition among American creative artists. Musicians and painters went there to study and to develop their talents in a climate that was more friendly and receptive to them. There were more opportunities for performances of their compositions and exhibitions of their paintings in Germany, England, Italy, and France than there were in the United States. To an even greater degree, American writers left their own land to work—or just to think—abroad. The list of authors who left the United States to work in what seemed to them the more favorable creative climate of Europe included some of the greatest names in American literature: Washington Irving, Nathaniel Hawthorne, James Fenimore Cooper, Edith Wharton, Henry James, Bret Harte, and Stephen Crane. Life in Europe not only encouraged them in their literary pursuits, it also gave them a perspective from which to view their own country.

This migration to Europe—temporary or permanent—continued through the first two decades of the twentieth century. In fact, during those years, three major American writers left their country forever: T. S. Eliot traveled to London; Ezra Pound went to London, Paris, and finally Italy; and Gertrude Stein took up permanent residence in France.

However, there has never been such a mass exodus of American intellectuals as there was during the years following the end of the First World War. Virtually every man and woman of importance in the American arts crossed the ocean and settled—for a short time, at least—in what was then the artistic capital of the world: Paris. For the greatest part of a decade, the capital of France was also the center of American intellectual life.

How did this happen? Why did Americans leave their country in droves? Why did they choose Paris rather than other European capitals? Just who were they and what did they do while in Paris? What were their accomplishments and what were their disappointments? And, finally, why did they return to their homes in the States?

This book is an attempt to answer these questions, to tell the story of this unique and exciting period—a part of American history, lived in a foreign capital. Just about every American writer, or would-be writer, who spent as much as a summer in Paris during the twenties has written of his or her experiences there. Putting all these reminiscences together would result in a volume several thousand pages long. Each man or woman remembers what he or she wants to; thus, in an anthology of these writings contradictions would abound, depending on the interpretation each author gives to the event that he or she experienced. The cast of characters in a story of this period is gigantic— in this book more names are omitted than included—and people pass in and out of the scene so quickly that any chronological telling of this story would be impossible. In addition, each man and woman, of necessity, lived a different day-to-day existence.

For these reasons, in order to give an accurate feeling of the life of Americans in Paris during the twenties, I have felt it best to present a collage of events and portraits. Through an account of the highlights of the decade and short portraits of its leading characters, we can most vividly get an overall impression of the times. The events described are both serious and lighthearted. Some are of lasting artistic importance—the opening of an important ballet, the premiere of an avant-garde symphonic work by a young American composer that stunned its French audience, the first public reading of selections from a novel that would be recognized as one of the great novels of the English language. Others are less serious but equally revealing as symbols of their times—a boxing match involving three important American writers and a glittering party on the river Seine.

Each section of this book reflects at least one aspect of this vital and colorful decade. Together they are meant to give the reader an idea of the special quality of the life lived by those Americans who experienced the world of Paris in the twenties.

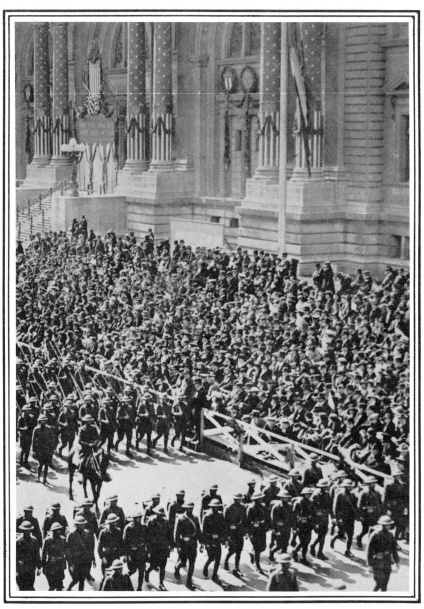

*Troops returning from France parade up Fifth Avenue past the
Metropolitan Museum of Art, New York City, 1919*

# Civilization in the United States

The climate in the United States after the end of World War One was such that it is not difficult to understand the need that many young Americans felt for escape and expatriation. During the war many hundreds of thousands of Americans had been sent overseas—and many others had volunteered their services as ambulance drivers—to take part in what was basically a bitter power struggle among the emerging national states of Europe. When the war came to a successful conclusion in 1918—with the United States and its European allies victorious—the Americans went home. A short-lived feeling of triumph soon turned to bitterness. A sense of patriotism, of purpose, had been instilled in the soldiers by wartime propaganda, but on reflection many of the returning soldiers realized it had been a useless war. More than 100,000 Americans had died in the course of the struggle, and a large number of the survivors felt that nothing had been accomplished.

Gertrude Stein called the generation that fought in the war the "Lost Generation," and indeed many of them did feel lost. At a time when they should have been choosing their professions and building their lives at home, they were off in foreign lands, fighting bloody battles for a cause they little understood.

On their return to their homes, they found conditions in the United States to be anything but encouraging. The economy was unstable and unemployment was rising in spite of an inflation that was giving Americans a false feeling of prosperity. There was disheartening political repression on a governmental level: anti-labor legislation led to a series of strikes that were brutally handled by management with the aid of police; strict immigration acts tended to seal off the country from the rest of the world by denying entry to all but a few aliens. The mood of the nation was restless and troubled, and to unite the people in a common cause, an enormous Red Scare was invented by A. Mitchell Palmer, an all-too-powerful attorney general who saw a threat of communism in every corner of American life and instigated massive raids to destroy this so-called threat to the country. On one single night in January 1920 he had

*U.S. Employment Service poster*

four thousand alleged political agitators arrested—and this was but one of the many infamous Palmer raids that threatened freedom of thought in the United States.

America's social habits, too, were being radically changed with the ratification of the Eighteenth Amendment to the Constitution, which prohibited the manufacture, sale, and transportation of alcoholic beverages. Prohibition continued, and as it did the sale and manufacture and transportation of alcohol fell into the hands and control of criminals, causing the inevitable rise in the rate of crime and corruption in the country.

Though the era of Prohibition was to last throughout the 1920s, the injustices triggered by the Red Scare came to a halt, labor strife diminished, and the American economy righted itself. The country was ready to go on the gaudy spree that F. Scott Fitzgerald had predicted. But it was an age of commercialism, of salesmanship, and of advertising, with little spiritual basis. Intellectuals were excluded; they felt the standards prevailing in the country were not their own. In some quarters there was open hostility to them, and in 1921 even Calvin Coolidge, who was to become President in 1923, declared that American universities were hotbeds of sedition.

Originality was not encouraged in the arts, and works of literature were subject to censorship by narrow-minded guardians of public morality. Of course, success was exalted even in the arts, but as the composer and critic Virgil Thomson wrote, "America was impatient with us, trying

*Front page stories record the anguish of a decade, from Mark Twain's death, through a war abroad, to increasing violence and disillusion at home, 1910–1920*

always to take us in hand and make us a success, or else squeezing us dry for exhibiting in an institution. America loved art but suspected distinction, stripped it off you every day for your own good."

F. Scott Fitzgerald, already a success in terms of fame and money, gave an even darker picture of the plight of the creative arts in America, writing, in 1925, to the essayist Marya Mannes:

"America's greatest promise is that something is going to happen, and after awhile you get tired of waiting because nothing happens to people except that they grow old, and nothing happens to American art because America is the story of the moon that never rose . . .

"America is so decadent that its brilliant children are damned almost before they are born."

The unhealthy climate of America after World War One described by Thomson and Fitzgerald was reflected by the publication in 1922 of *Civilization in the United States*, a symposium of thirty American intellectuals. The general editor of the slim volume was a thirty-one-year-old Harvard graduate named Harold Stearns. In an earlier book, *America and the Young Intellectual*, Stearns had given warning of the tone of his symposium by writing that the post-World War One generation "*does* dislike, almost to the point of hatred and certainly to the point of contempt,

*Harold Stearns*

the type of people who dominate in our present civilization."

The contributors to *Civilization in the United States* generally echoed Stearns's harsh views. Among them were distinguished professors of literature, Robert Morss Lovett and John Macy; an economist, George Soule; a music critic, Deems Taylor; a writer on city planning and architecture, Lewis Mumford; an expert on labor relations, Leo Wolman; a literary historian and essayist, Van Wyck Brooks; a brilliant social critic, H. L. Mencken; and a poet, Conrad Aiken. These were not young angry revolutionaries—most of them were over thirty years old, and some were in their forties and fifties. They were sober-minded, serious men, none of them connected with radical political movements and none, according to Stearns, were "martyrs" or "merely disgruntled."

Yet they generally agreed that civilization in the United States was at a low point. In their essays they criticized every facet of American life: politics, art, humor, journalism, medicine, scholarship, advertising, and theatre. (A rare exception was Conrad Aiken, who found a refreshing vitality in American poetry.) One contributor, Frank M. Colby, in his piece on American humor, reached the conclusion that there really was no such thing at all.

"The most amusing and pathetic fact in the social life of America today," wrote Stearns, "is its emotional and aesthetic starvation." Civilization was machine-made and standardized, and mediocrity was triumphant throughout the United States. The overall climate was not conducive to the development of the arts; original talent, though it did indeed exist, was not welcomed or rewarded. Life in America lacked spiritual depth and was joyless and colorless. There seemed to be no solution for a gifted American in his own country, and Harold Stearns felt that in order to flourish, the American intellectual had to flee his own land and settle in Europe where people knew how to live.

On July 4, 1921—his *own* independence day—Harold Stearns practiced what he had preached. After writing his preface to the symposium, he turned the entire manuscript in to the publisher and sailed for Europe.

Stearns's despair over the state of American culture was undoubtedly exaggerated, and his influence was not far-reaching. He was not the first American of the postwar generation to feel the need to escape to Europe, nor was his book very widely read. Yet his book and his expatriation to the Old World were symptomatic of a malaise that was spreading among a large number of young Americans —primarily those in the arts—during the years that followed the end of World War One. For a number of reasons they felt they could best develop their talents away from their own country.

The idea of going to Europe might not have occurred to so many Americans if it had not been for World War One. During that war those who had gone overseas had their first glimpse of another world and a different way of life. Europe was a world that, before the war, they had hardly been aware of, since America had, up to that time, been isolationist in mood, and Americans had, for the most part, been preoccupied with building their own young country. For the expatriates-to-be the Old World was a new world, and an attractive one.

On their leaves of absence, away from the front lines, the American soldiers and ambulance drivers went to the cities and liked what they saw. Even under the adverse conditions of wartime, they enjoyed and felt stimulated by their contacts with other cultures. Europe, they felt sure, had something special to offer them. So, feeling restless, discontented, and even unwanted by their own country after the war, many Americans once again crossed the ocean to settle in Europe. And in Europe, the one city that held the greatest appeal, that offered the greatest opportunity for both pleasure and development in the arts, was Paris.

# 2

# *A Kind of Extraordinary Rendezvous*

"There was something almost indescribably magnetic about Paris at the time," wrote Maria Jolas, one of the most distinguished American literary figures in the French capital during the twenties. "A kind of extraordinary rendezvous that everybody seemed to have come to almost without realizing it."

The enchanting City of Lights, with its wide tree-lined boulevards, its colorful outdoor markets, and its historical monuments, its winding river Seine, which divides the city into the Left Bank and the Right Bank—Paris was the logical setting for that rendezvous. More than any other city in the world during the 1920s it offered the right climate for an artist, musician, or writer. "Paris was," as

*Paris in the 1920s*

Gertrude Stein said, "where the twentieth century was . . . the place that suited those of us that were to create the twentieth century art and literature."

Paris was indeed the city that was witnessing the birth of all new fashions in art and literature. Before the war there was the revolution in art called Cubism, led by Pablo Picasso and Georges Braque, infusing the city with the excitement of a new discovery. Music and painting and dance were integrated in an altogether new way with the many appearances in the French capital of the Russian Ballet, led by Sergei Diaghilev, who brought together the greatest artists in all three fields—among them Picasso, the great composer Igor Stravinsky, and the magnificent dancer Nijinsky—and gave Paris's cultural life an unprecedented vitality. Paris welcomed the new and the experimental.

After the war ended, and during the 1920s, the greatest foreign writers, painters, and musicians took advantage of Paris's welcome and came to live and work there. Among the English-language writers, there was James Joyce. It was in Paris that he wrote *Finnegans Wake,* just as Gertrude Stein worked out her fascinating and controversial literary experiments in the French capital. And it was from his Parisian experiences that Ernest Hemingway was able to create his first successful novel, *The Sun Also Rises.* Though their contacts with their French colleagues were usually not frequent, these writers were working in the same atmosphere as such outstanding writers as Jean Cocteau, Louis Aragon, André Breton, Paul Valéry, and André Gide. Undeniably, as Harold Stearns wrote, they were "touched by the spiritual forces of French life."

Because France was not burdened by rigid censorship laws, and because they were writing in a language other

*Sergei Diaghilev*

than French, English-speaking writers were able to have books published in France that would have been banned or censored in the United States or England. In addition, their shorter uncommercial avant-garde works were published in English-language magazines, not only because there was greater freedom of expression but also because the cost of printing a book or magazine was far lower on the Continent. Quite simply, writers could work in a community of writers and with all the stimulation that that implies; there were also far greater chances that their works could reach the public for which they were meant. These conditions prevailed in other European countries—above all, Italy and Germany—but there was a magic quality about Paris, its remarkable physical beauty as well as its tradition of bohemianism, that drew writers to it.

Paris was even more advantageous for a musician. In America there was little or no chance of having a new composition performed. The public was not yet educated to the latest developments in the world of music; there was absolutely no taste for experimentation. During the season of 1925–1926 there were 3,394 musical performances in Paris while there were 1,156 in New York. Igor Stravinsky had settled in France after the war where, he felt, "the pulse of the world was throbbing most strongly." Naturally, the

*Igor Stravinsky, Nadia Boulanger, Darius Milhaud, and an un-identified woman*

disciples of the great master followed. In addition, the great teacher Nadia Boulanger lived in Paris; she was to influence generations of musicians, performers, and composers alike, among them the Americans Virgil Thomson and Aaron Copland. Also in Paris was a new and vital school of French composers—Arthur Honegger, Darius Milhaud, Francis Poulenc, and Erik Satie.

Young painters, too, could find a more suitable climate in Paris than in any other city for their growth. Foreign painters had come from all over the world—Picasso and Joan Miró from Spain, Marc Chagall from Russia, Constantin Brancusi from Rumania, Amedeo Modigliani from Italy. Art galleries were flourishing, and the possibilities for a painter or sculptor to find a place in which to exhibit his work were far more varied than they would have been elsewhere.

For all these reasons it was natural for young and gifted Americans to arrive in large numbers—not only as a negative move to flee from what they felt was an unhealthy climate, but as a positive move to take advantage of the benefits they could gain from a stay in Paris. Not only that: they had every reason to believe that the way of life was gentler and more pleasant in the French capital. As the American poet e.e. cummings wrote: "Paris (in each shape and gesture and avenue and cranny of her being) was continually expressing the humanness of humanity." The very beauty of the city attracted those with eyes sensitive enough to see beauty and be moved and influenced by it.

For economic reasons, too, the Americans came. Transatlantic fares were lower than ever, and the value of the dollar was higher than ever compared to the failing French franc. Rooms, studios, apartments, houses were easy to find at far lower rents than they would have cost in New

*Pablo Picasso in St. Raphael, 1919*

York. Food, too: for less than the equivalent of one dollar, one could dine reasonably well, and reasonably well in Paris meant very well back home. The fresh bread with its crisp crust; the endless variety of cheeses; and the inevitable and very inexpensive bottle of good wine. All in all, it was the quality of life in Paris that attracted visitors —good living, good eating, good drinking in a world that not only tolerated writers and painters and musicians but honored them, that respected their artistic experiments, and let the artist live and create in freedom.

Freedom, not only artistic but personal as well, counted. "Paris was the new frontier," wrote the Canadian author Morley Callaghan, "a promise of some enlargement of inner freedom." It was the freedom to dress as you please and drink as much as you please and keep the hours that best suited you and have the lover or lovers you wanted— and it was the freedom to grow.

Paris was everything. For some visitors it was a powerful majestic city, a city that stayed open all night and offered more pleasures than you could have at home. For these visitors the center was the fabulous Pigalle, with its dance halls and cabarets and burlesque shows. This was Gay Paree, as the tourists called it, where the women were beautiful and wild and the fun uninhibited.

But the artist's Paris was different: it was a series of

villages, of narrow winding streets lined with colorful bakeries, their sweets temptingly displayed; butcher shops with huge pieces of meat hanging from hooks; and fruit and vegetable stalls whose arrangements were works of art in themselves.

The village that the writers and painters and musicians made their own was called Montparnasse, on Paris's Left Bank; and the center of life in Montparnasse was its cafés. There were cafés to be found throughout Europe at the time—as meeting places they were very much a center of social activity—but none had the charm and none assumed the unique importance to the life of a city to as great an extent as did those of Montparnasse during the twenties.

# 3

# The Heart and Nervous System

When the eighteen-year-old John Glassco, a Canadian
determined to write his memoirs (which he did under the
title *Memoirs of Montparnasse*) and become a poet, arrived in Paris in 1928, the first thing he and his traveling
companion Graeme Taylor did was to head for those Montparnasse cafés. For a full week the two romantic young
men did little but wander from café to café, absorbing the
atmosphere and getting to know the people of the Parisian
quarter that was to be their temporary home.

Most newly arrived Americans did the same thing, for
the cafés were, as Malcolm Cowley who was there and
became the best historian of the period, wrote, "the heart
and nervous system of the American literary colony." For

*Malcolm Cowley*

another valuable chronicler of the times, Matthew Josephson, "the terraces of the Montparnasse cafés giving on the
lively Paris street scene were our 'university' during an
important stage of our lives."

In the early years of the twenties three cafés, all of them
on the wide tree-lined boulevard Montparnasse, attracted
the greatest crowds, "flowing out into the sidewalks," as
one observer George Antheil described them, "flouncing
awnings above them as risqué and lacy as a Victorian lady's
petticoat." One was the Rotonde, founded in 1911, on the
corner of the bustling boulevard Montparnasse and the
equally wide boulevard Raspail, a majestic street that had
just been inaugurated by France's President Poincaré. The
Rotonde was the headquarters of the bearded Russian revolutionaries in Paris—Lenin and Trotsky. It was largely
frequented by Mediterraneans and Slavs and by such
painters as Diego Rivera the Mexican, Modigliani the
Italian, Picasso the Spaniard, and Soutine the Lithuanian,
as well as the literary figures Apollinaire, Max Jacob, and
André Salmon. They were all great names but by the time
the Americans arrived in the twenties, most of them had
disappeared from the Montparnasse scene.

Next to the Rotonde was the Sélect, which set up its
first tables in 1924 and played host throughout the twenties
to both Americans and Central European painters. The

*The Dome*

café was presided over with stern efficiency by Madame Sélect, a formidable, large-bosomed woman with shrewd eyes whose fingerless mittens covered hands that worked away behind the cashier's desk while her husband, sporting a long drooping moustache, made Welsh rarebits.

Across the boulevard from the Rotonde and the Sélect was the oldest and most heavily frequented café of all— the Dôme. This venerable café was reputed to have been depicted in at least fifty novels written in fifteen languages, including Hemingway's *The Sun Also Rises*. In its early years in the nineteenth century it consisted of a simple zinc bar with a small terrace. By the twenties it had expanded into rows of tables and chairs that stretched out to the edge of the street; it was as crowded at two in the morning as it was at seven in the evening. It was undeniably the favorite of the Americans who filled its terrace day and night. "It was," wrote Geoffrey Fraser in the Paris *Tribune*, "not a place: it is an atmosphere, and no one has ever succeeded in describing an atmosphere. It may be felt, it may be absorbed, and you may, with the aid of a sensitive ear and a surreptitious pencil, record some of its concrete if fleeting manifestations." But that was all that could be done to convey the feeling of the Dôme.

All cafés played a central role in French society. For

Parisians, unwilling to offer the hospitality of their homes to all but their closest friends and relatives, they were the accepted meeting places in which to entertain. For the homeless Americans, the Montparnasse cafés to which they gravitated were more than that. They replaced the homes they had not found or could not afford in a foreign city. They became their unofficial headquarters, places where they were sure to meet someone familiar—or even unfamiliar—to keep them company. For the price of a cup of coffee, a man or woman could sit at a table for hours and learn the latest gossip, find a lead to an apartment, or a source from whom to borrow money. Those without money might find an invitation to dinner, and those lonely ones with money might find companionship. There was much talk, and the topics of conversation varied: life, sex, girlfriends, boyfriends, Joyce, Stein, soul, art, America, the latest fad. . . .

The cafés too were significant as places where one might be seen and see. Passing in front of the outdoor tables was an ever-fascinating cross section of Parisian life: prostitutes, models, newspaper vendors, flower girls, and Arab peddlers selling colorful rugs. Then, too, there was always the chance of an occasional celebrity: Raymond Duncan, brother of the famous dancer Isadora, might sweep by in his flowing Grecian robe; a Model T Ford carrying the

*e. e. cummings*

*John Dos Passos*

legendary Gertrude Stein and the ever-faithful Alice B. Toklas could well be puffing its way down the boulevard; at times, Ezra Pound, the great poet, could be seen hurrying by, as could the fabulous Kiki, the beautiful artists' model and cabaret singer, called the Queen of Montparnasse and known for her eccentric habits, her bizarre makeup, and her magnetic charm—as well as for the many men in her life, chief of whom during the twenties was the American expatriate Man Ray, who started as a painter and made his name as one of the great original photographers of this century.

But to see celebrities, it wasn't necessary to watch the passing crowds; there were enough of them seated at the Dôme or Sélect or Rotonde. A visitor might well get a glimpse of Sinclair Lewis, disapproving of the scene yet passing through it, or e.e. cummings or John Dos Passos —all major figures in the American literature of this century. At one table one might spy Ernest Hemingway and Jules Pascin, the painter; or on another night Hemingway might be deep in conversation with the Canadian Morley Callaghan. Michael Arlen, the author of the great best seller *The Green Hat,* might be seen at the Dôme, as might the talented author Kay Boyle or another most interesting woman writer, Djuna Barnes. Perhaps Edward

Titus might be there, with or without his wife Helena Rubinstein—Titus published a little magazine, and it would be easier to find a promising author at a café than it would be by mail. At another table there was a chance of finding the young, handsome, and glamorous Laurence Vail, with his long yellow hair and his pink or red shorts, accompanied by his wife the heiress Peggy Guggenheim who called her regal husband "the King of Bohemia."

Harold Stearns, too, was a habitué of the cafés, a familiar figure, stocky and unshaven, sometimes seated at a table and other times standing at the bar, often in a brown felt hat, wearing a dirty white shirt with frayed collars and a black business suit—"a shabby parody of respectability," as Kay Boyle called him. The enigmatic figure, whose collection of essays had summed up the discontent of Americans with their society, earned the money to pay for his drinks not through art or literature but through a racing column that he wrote for the Paris *Tribune* under the name of Peter Pickem. At the newspaper he was called the Hippique Buddha; he loved horses and would spend his days at the races, return to the paper to write his stories, and go on to Montparnasse where he would drink until dawn. He was a man of intelligence, and his knowledge of French literature was profound, but as a semidrunken figure who spent his nights at the bars of Montparnasse he was ridiculed. "There," the tourists would say, pointing to him, "is civilization in the United States."

Another familiar figure seen at the Dôme or the Sélect was a slender, nervous, straight-nosed young man with intense, curious blue eyes named Robert McAlmon. It was McAlmon who always had the latest gossip, who knew where everyone was and what everyone was doing. In one way or another he was connected with all the major and many of the minor figures who passed through Paris in the twenties.

Born in a small Kansas town in 1896, the son of a minister, McAlmon worked his way across the country as a dishwasher and as a model for painters and sculptors. In New York he met Annie Winifred Ellerman, a shy blue-eyed English girl. The next day they were married, and McAlmon's fortune was made, for his wife (who later wrote successful books under the name Bryher) was the daughter of a shipping magnate, one of England's richest men. The marriage lasted not much longer than the courtship had, but McAlmon profited from it enormously. He was thereafter called, contemptuously, Robert McAlimony, a reference to the large sums of money that his wife's father gave to him, and he settled in the more congenial climate of Europe. There he spent his fortune on a new publishing house, Contact Editions, which published Hemingway and

*Robert McAlmon*

Stein among others. He was unfailingly generous to young writers, helping them find publishers for their works as well as aiding them financially when necessary. He was a writer himself—and many serious critics admired his writing—but he was too busy socially to pursue his own career successfully. But he was laughed at for his writing, too, and someone wrote of him: "I'd rather live in Oregon and pack salmon, than live in Nice and write like Robert McAlmon." He had his enemies like Hemingway and Fitzgerald—the latter called him "a bitter rat"—but he also had staunch supporters. He was, according to William Bird, his associate at Contact Editions, "exploited, betrayed, neglected, deceived and imitated beyond recognition." And Kay Boyle, who admired the writer as well as the man, wrote that "in the complex role of prolific writer, generous publisher, ruthless critic, exuberant drinker and dancer, outspoken enemy of the sham, skeptical friend of Joyce, Pound, Katherine Anne Porter and countless other writers, there was never anyone quite like McAlmon around."

*Everyone* was indeed at the cafés, and yet not really everyone. Gertrude Stein stayed at home, and Stravinsky had too much work to do. James Joyce and Ezra Pound appeared rarely and only for specific appointments. Hemingway, too, would sit on a terrace only after his work was done. For him and for the other hardworking writers and painters who had come to Paris, these undeniably pleasant meeting places served for conversation and relaxation and a change of pace, but for many American expatriates, café-sitting became a full-time occupation. Though they might have come to Paris to work, these latter, seduced by the attractive Parisian way of life and insufficiently motivated to create, lived their lives at the cafés. Understandably, they drew the wrath of those men and women who actually did work in Paris.

"The scum of Greenwich Village, New York, has been skimmed off and deposited in large ladlesful on that section of Paris adjacent to the Café Rotonde," Hemingway reported bitterly in the Toronto *Star Weekly* of March 25, 1922.

They have all striven so hard for a careless individuality of clothing that they have achieved a sort of uniformity of eccentricity. A first look into the smoky, high-ceilinged, table-crammed interior of the Rotonde gives you the same feeling that hits you as you step into the bird house of the zoo. There seems to be a tremendous, raucous, many-pitched squawking going on broken up by many waiters who fly around through the smoke like so many black and white magpies. The tables are full—they are always full—someone is moved down and crowded together, something is knocked over, more people come in at the swinging door, another black and white waiter pivots between tables toward the door and, having shouted your order at his disappearing back, you look around at individual people.

The gang that congregates at the corner of the Boulevard Montparnasse and the Boulevard Raspail have no time to work at anything else; they put in a full day at the Rotonde.

Elliot Paul, a critic, editor, and novelist who lived in Paris for many years, also had few kind words for the café-dwellers. "They have dark circles under their eyes, have read parts of *Ulysses,* and are likely to be self-made Freudians. They speak most impressively when they are vague and most erratically when they seek to be specific. They hate to spend money for either food or clothes." Alex Small of the Paris *Tribune* also found their so-called intellectual conversations a fraud.

There was one sort of conversation in which the Montparnassians excelled. That was gossip and personalities. It began usually with the autobiographer, and the hapless victim of the monologue would be lucky if he could escape without hearing all about the amorous, intellectual, and spiritual life of the talker. . . . Everyone who came to Montparnasse had the passion for explaining himself.

Obviously, there is much truth in what these three writers had to say about the regulars at the Montparnasse cafés, but there is also truth in the statement of the journalist Bruce Bliven that "it may well be the case that of ten

Latin Quarter aesthetes, one genuine artist may be produced. It may also be true that this one artist has a real need for the sort of life the Left Bank offers. In that case, the nine who provide the milieu may well be excused for the sake of the tenth."

Much can be written for and against the life led at the cafés of Montparnasse, but they were unquestionably a vital part of the lives of most of the expatriates who were drawn to Paris during the twenties. There was nothing like them at home, and it was along the terraces of the boulevard Montparnasse that most of the Americans were not only introduced to the people but to the special atmosphere that would forever remain a part of their experience.

# 4

# *In the Mature Gertrudian Bosom*

Paris had many wondrous sights in addition to the cafés—there were museums and palaces and the Eiffel Tower. Yet, for an American visitor interested in the arts, on the top of the list was the home of Gertrude Stein.

An American who had come to Paris in 1903, she was already a legend by the early 1920s. She had discovered and championed the cause of the greatest painter of the time—Pablo Picasso. She had written puzzling, often incomprehensible books, books that were noteworthy because she used the English language in a new way. Her work was little read, though it was widely talked about, but the fame of the solidly built, squat woman had spread throughout the world, and her salon at 27 rue de Fleurus was a must for every aspiring writer.

*Gertrude Stein*

*Gertrude Stein and Alice B. Toklas in their apartment at 27 rue de Fleurus*

It was on Saturday evening that she held court, and a court it really seemed, with the blue-eyed hostess fully in charge of the proceedings. Because of her noble, finely shaped head, with grizzled, short-cropped hair, many writers have described her as resembling a Roman emperor; and she played the role, attended by a small, thin wiry woman named Alice B. Toklas who had been her intimate friend since 1907 and would be so for the rest of her life.

The setting for Gertrude Stein's salon was an enormous and somewhat somber studio. Heated by a huge iron stove, it was filled with heavy pieces of Italian Renaissance furniture and cumbersome chairs on which the awed visitors sat uncomfortably. The guests were, for the most part, soberly dressed, as for a command appearance at court. They were dazzled by the magnificent collection of paintings that hung two and three deep on the walls of the vast room—works by modern masters like Picasso (his portrait of the hostess was prominently displayed), Braque, and Juan Gris, whom Gertrude Stein had discovered before they were well known. And they were subdued by the overwhelming presence and strength of personality of Gertrude Stein—her every word was eagerly awaited, her warm hearty laughter completely charmed the assembled group of admirers.

They were not all admirers, however. A strong-willed woman, with a healthy sense of her own importance, she had definite opinions that were unshakable. Because of this, she made as many enemies as she made friends, and often the latter turned into the former. Nonetheless, as Van Wyck Brooks wrote, American writers in Paris highly valued an invitation to come to the studio at 27 rue de Fleurus to take refuge "in the mature Gertrudian bosom, much like that of their prairie mother, but of a gratifying

*Juan Gris*

sophistication . . . they had fine, babbling times together."

Not every visitor, of course, had a fine time—Gertrude Stein's disapproval could be quick, final, and devastating. Young John Glassco came as an uninvited guest—through a friend—and found the atmosphere "almost ecclesiastical." He was taken aback by the formidable physical appearance of his hostess, "who was presiding like a Buddha at the far end of the room." Obviously not entering into the spirit of the salon, and making matters worse by disagreeing with his hostess on the merits of Jane Austen (he liked her; she didn't), he was abruptly asked to leave the party by one of Gertrude's faithful male attendants.

Glassco was not alone in being in Gertrude Stein's disfavor. When she first met the great poet Ezra Pound, she rather liked him but didn't find him "amusing." Their second meeting, however, was their last. Pound talked about subjects that bored Gertrude and had the presumption to explain the meanings of paintings that hung on *her* walls. His compulsive talking and general nervousness irritated her, but the final straw came when, in a state of violent excitement, he fell out of her favorite armchair. That was it. The aggressive, high-strung, self-confident poet was never again invited to the Stein residence. She characterized him as a "village explainer," which meant that his conversation was "excellent if you were a village, but if you were not, not." His opinion of her was even less kind—he described her to friends as a parasite and called her "an old tub of guts."

The novelist Glenway Wescott, too, did not come up to Gertrude Stein's standards. He was abruptly dismissed as having "a certain syrup, but it does not pour."

Nonetheless, when Gertrude approved of a writer and admired his work, her enthusiasm knew no bounds. Her profound interest in the craft of writing and the importance she attached to the uses of language were of tremendous help to three major American writers, two of whom became her lifelong friends.

One of these was Sherwood Anderson, who looked her up when he came to Paris in 1921. Anderson was in no way an expatriate, nor was he a young man. His past was an unusual one, for he had been a respectable and successful Ohio businessman, with a wife and children, who had suffered a nervous breakdown while in his late thirties. Entirely changing the course of his life, he left his job and family and went off to Chicago to write a novel. That novel was not published until he was already forty years old. He was forty-five when he first met Gertrude Stein.

Their meeting was a complete success. Alice B. Toklas, undoubtedly speaking for Gertrude as well as for herself, found he showed a "winning brusquerie, a mordant wit

*Sherwood Anderson*

and an all-inclusive heart." And Anderson, for his part, was equally taken by Gertrude's health and strength and laughter. "She tells stories with an American shrewdness in getting the tang and the kick into the telling," he wrote in his notebook.

He admired her writing as well and admitted to being influenced by it. "Miss Stein is a worker in words with the same loving touch in her strong fingers that was characteristic of the women of the kitchens of the old brick houses in the town of my boyhood . . . in her own great kitchen she is making something with her materials, something sweet to the tongue and fragrant to the nostrils," he noted.

Gertrude Stein, up to that time, had had little serious encouragement as a writer. Her fame and notoriety rested on her art collection and her extraordinary personality; as a writer she had been more mocked than praised. Because of this, she was especially moved by Anderson's intelligent and sensitive appraisal of her work. "I don't think you quite realize what it meant," she wrote him, "to have some one and you have been the only one quite simply to understand what it is all about simply understand as any one would suppose everyone would understand and to so charmingly and directly tell it to me."

She, too, was enthusiastic about Anderson's writing and gave him good advice. "You know some day Sherwood you must write a novel that is just one portrait. You are a peach of a portraitist to sometime do a novel that is just one portrait and nobody else's feelings coming in."

The author of *Winesburg, Ohio* stayed in Paris a short time, but throughout his lifetime he continued to correspond with Gertrude Stein. "Gee I love you," he wrote her; "I can't tell you how much you always mean to me," she answered him.

An equally warm relationship developed between Gertrude and F. Scott Fitzgerald. When Fitzgerald came to Paris, he was young, handsome, and intelligent, already renowned for his charm and wit. Unlike the other young Americans who came to the rue de Fleurus, he was already an established success, his first novel, *This Side of Paradise,* having brought him fame and fortune when he was just twenty-four years old.

Gertrude had read it and had recognized the young writer's enormous talent. "It was this book that really created the public for the new generation," she wrote. For her, Fitzgerald was "the first of the lost generation . . . the only one at that time of their descent on Paris to have already given proof of a gift."

The two writers got along beautifully at once, and young Fitzgerald was as enthusiastic about Gertrude's writing as

*F. Scott Fitzgerald*

she was about his. He was most anxious to read the manuscript of *The Making of Americans,* a gigantic novel she had been working on for years, and one for which she was finding it impossible to get a publisher. "I am so anxious to get The Making of Americans & learn something from it and imitate things out of it which I shall doubtless do," Fitzgerald wrote her. When he read the manuscript, he was fascinated, and he, too, tried in vain to have it published in America. He was shocked that there was no publisher courageous enough to undertake its publication. "I thought," he wrote, "it was one purpose of critics and publishers to educate the people up to original work."

Fitzgerald and Stein remained friends throughout their lifetimes, just as Gertrude did with Sherwood Anderson. Between them there were no significant quarrels. There was, however, one other American writer whose work she greatly influenced and with whom she had a far stormier and more complicated relationship. His name was Ernest Hemingway.

# 5

# If You're a Writer, You Write

"If you're a writer, you write," said Ernest Hemingway, and that's just what he came to Paris to do. More than any other writer, his name is today identified with the young Americans in Paris during the twenties. He spent most of the first half of that period in the French capital and immortalized its mood and its people in one of his most successful novels, *The Sun Also Rises.*

He was born in Oak Park, Illinois, in 1899. At the age of nineteen, he was a cub reporter for the Kansas City *Star* and soon after that volunteered his services as an ambulance driver during World War One. He was known for his toughness and courage and was passionately interested in sports—participating in them as well as watching them.

*Ernest Hemingway*

His thirst for adventure and excitement almost cost him his life; he was seriously wounded on the Italian front.

When the war ended, he went to Canada, to Toronto,

where he wrote feature stories for the Toronto *Star Weekly*. But his heart wasn't in journalism; his heart was set on becoming a creative writer.

Not long afterward, he had dinner with Sherwood Anderson, who had just returned from his stay in Paris. He had glowing reports of the life of the artist in the French capital and convinced Hemingway that Paris was the best place for a serious writer to pursue his career. A few days after Thanksgiving of 1921, Hemingway sailed for France—with his beautiful new wife Hadley, and with a letter of introduction to Gertrude Stein. Though he was only twenty-two years old, unknown and unpublished, Anderson wrote his friend that Hemingway was "a writer instinctively in touch with everything worthwhile in the United States."

The first thing Ernest and Hadley did after their arrival in Paris was to look for an apartment, and they soon found one on the rue du Cardinal Lemoine, in the midst of a lively, colorful working-class district. Hemingway badly needed a base from which to write, but the apartment was so small and crowded that he had to rent a hotel room in which to work. Money was tight, and the young couple at first had to live on practically nothing. Their lunches usually consisted of an egg, a glass of wine, and usually a boiled potato. However, no sacrifice was great enough for

Hemingway as long as he would be able to devote his time to creative writing. To bring in some money, he had to continue doing assignments for the Toronto newspaper, but he hoped to keep these at a minimum.

He loved Paris and felt at home there; the village atmosphere of his neighborhood, its sights and smells, delighted him, and he was inspired by the paintings he saw in the museums, paintings which in some ways would guide him in his own work. He stayed away from the literary cafés as much as possible, going there only for specific appointments. He had nothing but contempt for the crowds that spent their days and nights sitting in Montparnasse and had no patience with their talk about art and artists. No one could write in a café, and he had come to Paris to write. He wanted to write. He wanted to develop his own style, to convey his meanings and emotions clearly and concisely, using the right words in the right order. Writing was a skill to be worked at and practiced.

Not until three months after his arrival in Paris did Hemingway have the courage to call on Gertrude Stein. But he needed no courage; Gertrude was immediately taken by his charm and warmth. This rather large young man, shy and yet self-confident, dressed in a patched jacket and wearing sneakers, disarmed her at once with his engaging smile. She found him "rather foreign-looking" and very handsome, with his deep black hair, small moustache, and dark intense eyes, which she found to be "passionately interested rather than interesting."

Hemingway, too, was immediately attracted to Gertrude Stein and her strong personality. Physically, she reminded him of a northern Italian peasant, and he felt at ease in her apartment. "There was a big fireplace, and it was warm and comfortable and they gave you good things to eat and there was tea and natural distilled liqueurs made from purple plums, yellow plums or wild raspberries," he later wrote.

The two spoke of their common passion for literature and the art of writing, and at the end of that first meeting the young man invited Gertrude and Alice B. Toklas to dine with him and his wife at their small apartment. The two women happily accepted the invitation, and Gertrude spent most of the time poring through everything Hemingway had written. She liked some things, and she didn't like others, but she instinctively foresaw a brilliant future for the young writer. The faults she found with his work were faults that he himself had sensed, and he listened attentively and appreciatively that evening and during the many long walks through Paris's Left Bank that followed.

The two became intimate friends, and Hemingway shared all his problems with the older woman—personal ones as well as professional ones. His need to earn money forced him to continue working for the newspaper, and far too many assignments took him away from Paris, but wherever he was he kept in touch with Gertrude Stein.

Not only was his journalism taking up too much of his time, but it was damaging him by keeping him away from Paris where he was happiest, where he was getting to know the people who could help him in his career—he and Ezra Pound, who encouraged so many young writers, had become friends—and he was beginning to make a name for himself in literary circles. He even had a promise of book publication—Robert McAlmon wanted to bring out a collection of his writings, *Three Stories and Ten Poems*. But he had a wife to feed and soon there would be a child, for Hadley was pregnant. It was impossible for him to devote enough time to Paris or to his own writing.

He turned to Gertrude Stein and presented her with his dilemma. She thoroughly sympathized and feared that the journalist in him—and he was a most skilled journalist— might well destroy the creative artist. Her advice was to return to Toronto, work as hard as he could for the newspaper so that he could accumulate enough money to return to Paris and concentrate on his writing. Hemingway agreed, and Hadley was pleased because she wanted the baby to be born in America.

The period in Canada was a restless one. Hemingway worked hard and successfully at his journalism, but he grew increasingly anxious to return to Paris. The baby was born, a boy, and after a while he wryly wrote to Gertrude to say that "I am getting very fond of him." He also wrote to say that when the baby, nicknamed Bumby, was three months old, he would give up journalism and the Hemingways would return to Paris.

In January 1924, he kept to his word and was back in Paris. The infant was baptized, and Gertrude and Alice were the joint godmothers. The friendship picked up where it had left off. Hemingway was in a good mood; he was optimistic. McAlmon was going ahead with his plans to publish one book, and Ezra Pound and William Bird, who had a small publishing house called Three Mountains Press, commissioned him to write another so that they, too, could introduce his work to the public. This latter book would be a collection of pieces entitled *in our time.*

On the brink of success and recognition, Hemingway still needed and sought Gertrude's help and approval, which she unfailingly gave to him. He came to her aid as well, arranging for a serialization of *The Making of Americans* in *Transatlantic Review,* a literary magazine directed by Ford Madox Ford, for which Hemingway served as assistant editor, reader, and scout. Not only did he arrange

SEPT FRANCS CINQUANTE

*the*

VOL. I. No. 4
April 1924

# transatlantic

*Edited in Paris*
*by* F. M. FORD

*review*

## CONTENTS

PARIS :
The Transatlantic Review Co., 29, Quai d'Anjou.
7 FRS. 50

NEW YORK :
Thomas Seltzer, Inc.
50 c.

LONDON :
Duckworth & Co.
2/-

for the publication of this difficult book, he also helped Gertrude copy out fifty pages of the only existing copy of the manuscript so that she might give one to the printer.

Nonetheless, the prospect of success seemed to change Hemingway. He quarreled with Ford Madox Ford and left the magazine. He became associated with another little magazine, but shortly thereafter quarreled with the editor and left that job. Even his relations with Hadley were cooling.

In 1925 he finally found a commercial American publisher for his books—the courageous Horace Liveright, who contracted to publish a volume of Hemingway's writing under the collective title *in our time*. Liveright's offer came just in time, as the young writer soon afterward had an offer from another perceptive editor, Maxwell Perkins, Scott Fitzgerald's editor at Scribner's, asking for a book of his. Hemingway hadn't met Fitzgerald yet—the latter called Perkins's attention to his work on the basis of what he had read—though the two were to become good friends.

It was during this period that Hemingway tried to write a novel; he had not, up to that time, felt comfortable in that longer form and was happier writing short pieces. This first attempt failed, and he soon abandoned it. "If you're a good writer, you write about things you know," he had said, and what he knew didn't work into a novel. But

*Maxwell Perkins*

finally, in the spring of 1925, he found his subject, and it was something that he knew. It was a story based on his own experiences during a trip to Spain, the third one he had made to Pamplona, where he had come to love the bullfights. He went there with friends from Paris, and he wrote about them, pulling no punches, inventing as all novelists must, but not disguising the characters sufficiently to spare the feelings of his models. On September 21, 1925, the novel was finished; he was physically and emotionally exhausted, but he had completed it to his own satisfaction.

A few weeks later Liveright published *in our time*. The reviews were good, but the critics kept comparing him to Sherwood Anderson, which he resented. He was Hemingway, not Anderson. In anger, he sat down to write a parody of a recently popular Anderson novel called *Dark Laughter*. Hemingway's novel was called *The Torrents of Spring,* and it bitterly made fun of Sherwood Anderson. By contract, Hemingway had to submit this new book to Horace Liveright, and he dutifully did so. But Anderson was Liveright's friend, as well as his best-selling author, and it was impossible for him to accept for publication a work that satirized Anderson. Because of this, Hemingway was free to give the book to Maxwell Perkins, who enthusiastically accepted it on behalf of Scribner's. Perkins, too, would publish Hemingway's other novel, about a group of American expatriates at a Spanish bullfight—*The Sun Also Rises.*

More of Hemingway's friendships came to an end, as did his marriage. When in October 1926 *The Sun Also Rises* was published, its contents offended some of those people who had befriended him, but its success made him famous. He was proud—but not unreasonably so—of his sudden fame, though it seemed to carry with it the end of many of his past associations, including his seemingly indestructible friendship with Gertrude Stein.

There was a break between them, and a sharp one, but the specific causes are unclear. Certainly Gertrude was upset by his attack on Sherwood Anderson, to whom she remained intensely loyal, and that was probably the beginning of the coolness that developed between the two writers. Another factor might well be that they simply had outgrown each other, did not need each other any longer. During the first years of their friendship, Hemingway glowingly acknowledged to one and all his debt to Gertrude Stein, both as a friend and a literary mentor. By the time *The Sun Also Rises* was published, he was so well known that he forgot—publicly at least—how much he had learned from his friend and how much she had helped him when he desperately needed encouragement. But the critics didn't forget; they kept reminding him of his literary and stylistic debt to Gertrude, and this embittered him toward her.

As for Gertrude Stein, she believed that not only had success changed him, but that because of it his writing had lost its early freshness. She wanted nothing more to do with him; she was as accustomed as he was to making good friends and then losing them. This was just one more example for each writer. Once, several years later, they met on a street and Hemingway said that he was rich and old and tired and wanted to resume their friendship. Coldly, she replied that she was none of those things and preferred to let matters stand as they were.

In time, they began to talk to others against each other and even to write against each other, thereby airing their feud in public. "He looks like a modern and he smells of the museums," Gertrude wrote of him contemptuously, and he responded by viciously parodying her style in some of his books. In her one commercial success, *The Autobiography of Alice B. Toklas,* published in 1933, she wrote that in spite of Hemingway's outward display of courage and daring, he was really "yellow." This infuriated him more than anything could, for it called into question his widely advertised virility, and he reacted bitterly. Gertrude Stein, he is reported to have told friends, had gone through three stages: first, she felt that anyone who was not homosexual was no good; then, she believed that all homosexuals were necessarily talented; and, finally, she concluded that no one was any good who was not homosexual. He dismissed *The Autobiography of Alice B. Toklas* as a "damned pitiful book."

In spite of this, until the end of her life Gertrude Stein admitted to a "weakness" for her old friend and protégé. Hemingway, however, seemed to harbor no such weakness for his old friend. In *A Moveable Feast,* a memoir of his Paris years published after his death, he writes bitterly about her. He qualifies his earlier enthusiasm for *The Making of Americans* and he gives unflattering versions of episodes in her life that contradict what other observers have written. Finally, he attacks her sexuality—for the first time in print—by recording an ugly lesbian quarrel between Gertrude and Alice that he claims to have overheard.

It is, of course, sad that such a mutually beneficial friendship came to such an end, but Paris in the twenties—a time of growth and development among artists—was the scene of many such friendships and many such quarrels.

## 6

# A Warm, Cheerful Place

Not everybody quarreled with everybody during those years, and Ernest Hemingway never had a serious disagreement with the other woman he went to see at the suggestion of Sherwood Anderson. Her name was Sylvia Beach, and she too was an American woman who had come to live in Paris.

This small woman with lively brown eyes and a somewhat masculine air was born in Princeton, New Jersey, in 1887. The daughter of a distinguished Presbyterian minister, she visited France often during her childhood and adolescence. She developed a love for the French people and their culture, and in 1917 she went to Paris to pursue her passionate interest in French literature. While there, her search for hard-to-find books led her to a small Left Bank bookshop owned by Adrienne Monnier. A buxom, stout woman, with a pink-and-white complexion, Adrienne Monnier greeted Sylvia warmly. She was impressed by her knowledge and interest in French literature, and the two women became friends at once. Sylvia joined Adrienne's La Société des Amis des Livres, which not only had a rental library service but also published a magazine, *Le Navire d'Argent,* and organized evenings to which members were invited to hear French authors read from their own works. Through this association Sylvia came to know the bookshop's steady customers and friends: Paul Valéry, André Gide, Paul Claudel, and André Breton—some of France's most important writers—as well as the musicians Milhaud, Honegger, and Poulenc. It was the ideal introduction to contemporary French culture for a young American woman.

Sylvia wanted to acquaint more Americans with this culture, and to do so she planned to open a bookshop in New York, the first such store to specialize in French literature. But the costs for such a venture were prohibitive, and she was forced to reverse her plans. Instead of a French bookshop in New York, she would open an American bookshop and lending library in Paris. In that way she would help the French become acquainted with the best and newest writing being done in the English language. It would

*Adrienne Monnier*

not be easy, but she had the guidance of Adrienne, an experienced bookseller, as well as her own boundless energy and enthusiasm.

Her first problem was to find a site for the bookshop, and in this Adrienne was a great help. The two women made an amusing pair, walking down the narrow Left Bank streets in search of suitable space: Sylvia inevitably dressed in a short skirt, a jacket covering a white blouse with a large collar and a large bow at her throat; and Adrienne, described by some as looking like a French milkmaid of the eighteenth century, in a long full gray skirt, a white silk blouse partially covered by a tight-fitting velveteen vest.

Before long, a location was found and, happily, it was very near Adrienne's own store (the shop moved to somewhat larger quarters around the corner two years later). The next problem was that of finding books and for this Sylvia scoured the secondhand shops of Paris; she also traveled to London and bought what she felt appropriate for the shop. In addition, her sister in New York helped out by ordering for her the latest and best American titles. Current best sellers interested her little; she wanted her bookshop to specialize in works by the modern masters— Yeats, Pound, and Joyce, above all. In the meantime carpenters got to work installing shelves and renovating the premises while Sylvia herself went about buying furniture, as inexpensively as possible, from the flea market.

Shakespeare and Company, as it was baptized, opened on November 19, 1919, on a colorful street behind the Palais du Luxembourg. In front of it, hanging from a bar above the entrance, was an old-fashioned painted signboard portrait of Shakespeare. On one side was written "Bookshop;" on the other, "Lending Library." Displayed in the

*Sylvia Beach*

window were those books dearest to Sylvia Beach—from Chaucer to Joyce.

The shop itself was divided into two rooms. In the front room the walls were lined with bookshelves stuffed with books, and in the back room there was a comfortable parlor, with a fireplace, where tea was served. Any available wall space was covered with photographs of authors of the past—Walt Whitman, Oscar Wilde, Edgar Allan Poe, and others—as well as those contemporary authors who would soon become Sylvia Beach's good friends.

The number of photographs of the latter grew steadily throughout the years. It didn't take long for Americans in Paris, especially writers, to realize that in Shakespeare and Company, as Hemingway said, they "had a warm, cheerful place" to come to, and in Sylvia Beach they had an intelligent, sympathetic, and helpful friend.

Among the first visitors to the shop were Ezra Pound, dressed in his usual velvet jacket and open-road shirt, and his wife Dorothy Shakespear Pound. The poet wanted to know if anything in the store was in need of repair, and Sylvia obliged him by putting him to work fixing a chair and a cigarette box. Mrs. Pound worried that customers would be unable to find the out-of-way shop and volunteered to draw a map that was printed on the back of the lending library circular. It was signed, appropriately, D. Shakespear.

*Ezra Pound at Shakespeare and Company, 1922*

Among other early customers were two rather unusual-looking women. "One of them, with a very fine face, was stout, wore a long robe, and, on her head, a most becoming top of a basket," Sylvia Beach wrote. "She was accompanied by a slim dark whimsical woman: she reminded me of a gypsy." They were, of course, Gertrude Stein and Alice B. Toklas. Gertrude complained that the shop lacked amusing titles such as the romantic novel *The Trail of the Lonesome Pine,* but she was still enthusiastic about both the store and its owner and was one of the first subscribers to its lending library. Not only that, she composed an advertisement that was sent out to other potential subscribers, which read: "Rich and Poor in English to Subscribers in French and Other Latin Tongues."

Before long, Shakespeare and Company became more than just a bookshop: it was a mailing address for the temporarily homeless, a bank in which to cash checks, and a club for members of the so-called Lost Generation to meet each other. The list of visitors to Sylvia's store included so many important literary figures that George Antheil, the young composer, was justified in calling it "the center of belles-lettres in the English language on the Continent."

Sylvia Beach ably describes some of these in her memoirs, *Shakespeare and Company.* There was John Dos

*Archibald MacLeish*

Passos, always busy and hurried; the ever-charming Scott
Fitzgerald; Kay Boyle, who wanted to work in the shop;
Archibald MacLeish, who became a close friend as did
Janet Flanner; the interesting Sherwood Anderson;
Stephen Vincent Benét, one of the earliest visitors; the
shy and polite Thornton Wilder; Djuna Barnes, a novelist
Sylvia particularly admired; Allen Tate, the brilliant poet
and critic . . .

All these, and very many others, became supporters and
devotees of this fascinating, unique bookshop, which was
fulfilling its owner's purpose in giving France a perceptive
look at American culture. But of them all, two of this
century's greatest writers were of more than special interest
to Sylvia Beach.

One was Ernest Hemingway. From the moment she met
him, Sylvia was enchanted by this tall rugged man with
the strangely high-pitched midwestern voice, just as Gertrude Stein had been—though Sylvia and Hemingway were
to remain friends throughout their lifetimes. Under his
surface toughness Sylvia found him sensitive, wise, and
extremely intelligent. He loved books as much as she did,
and he also taught her to enjoy watching those sporting
events so dear to him. He invited Sylvia and Adrienne to
boxing matches and bicycle races to which they responded
enthusiastically. He read aloud parts of *in our time,* which

Who is Sylvia, what is she
That all our scribes commend her?
Yankee, young and brave is she
The ~~West~~ ~~this~~ west this grace did lend her
That all books might published be.

Is she rich as she is brave
For wealth oft daring misses?
those
~~Though~~ about her rant and rave
To subscribe for Ulysses
But, having signed, they ponder grave.

Then to Sylvia let us sing
Her daring lies in selling.
She can sell each mortal thing
That's boring beyond telling.
To her let us buyers bring.

                              J. J.
                              after
                              W. S.

*A poem written by James Joyce for Sylvia Beach*

confirmed their feeling that he was a most gifted writer, and he made frequent visits to the shop with his young child Bumby, even before the latter could walk.

Hemingway remained enthusiastic about his friend Sylvia Beach, and in *A Moveable Feast* he wrote: "She was kind, cheerful and interested, and loved to make jokes and gossip. No one that I ever knew was nicer to me."

But it was another writer who changed Sylvia Beach's life, who became a cause for her—and a worthwhile one—James Joyce. When hopes for publication of his masterpiece *Ulysses* seemed dim because of absurd and thoroughly outdated censorship laws, it was Sylvia Beach who courageously, and at great personal sacrifice, came to the rescue. She became not only the brilliant Irishman's publisher, but his secretary, manager, and close friend as well. For several years Shakespeare and Company was James Joyce's office, his publishing house, and his second home.

# 7

# A Simple Middle-Class Man

He called himself "a simple middle-class man," but James Joyce was the giant who towered over all other literary figures during the 1920s. It was in Paris that he finished one masterpiece, *Ulysses*, and began work on another, *Finnegans Wake*. The publication of the former, according to Janet Flanner in *The New Yorker,* "was indubitably the most exciting, important, historic single literary event of the early Paris expatriate literary colony." According to Richard Ellman, author of a superlative biography of Joyce, "to have read *Ulysses,* or parts of it, became the mark of the knowledgeable expatriate."

James Joyce was born outside Dublin on February 2, 1882, one of ten children. By the time he had finished his

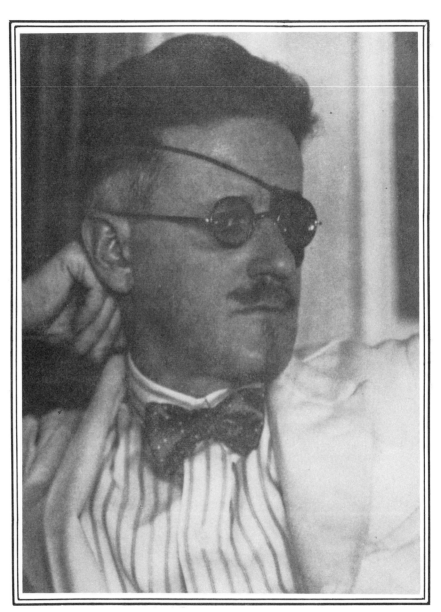

*James Joyce*

studies at the university in 1902, he had completely re-
belled against his family's environment, his religion, and
his country, Ireland. After living in Paris for a year, he
returned to Dublin in 1903, but the following year he left
Ireland forever, taking with him a strikingly beautiful
but simple and poorly educated young woman named Nora
Barnacle, who would never understand his writing but on
whom he was to be completely dependent for the rest of his
life. (They married in 1931.) From 1905 to 1915 they
lived in Trieste, Italy, where the brilliant Irishman barely
made a living by teaching English while at the same time
completing *Dubliners,* a collection of fifteen short stories,
and writing his first novel, the autobiographical *A Portrait
of the Artist as a Young Man.*

During World War One, Joyce left Italy for Zurich,
Switzerland, where he began work on *Ulysses,* which would
later be considered by many the greatest novel of this century. When the war came to an end, he moved to Paris
where he and Nora and their two children arrived on July
8, 1920. They were to stay there for twenty years.

When James Joyce arrived in the French capital, his
work was already well known, but his earnings were next
to nothing. Ezra Pound took charge—he had early recognized Joyce's genius and had arranged for the publication

*Sylvia Beach and James Joyce*

of *A Portrait of the Artist as a Young Man* in the British magazine *The Egoist*. The American poet found Joyce a place to live temporarily, introduced him to important figures in Parisian and expatriate literary circles, and helped him out by giving him as much money as he could. In spite of his reputation as a writer of enormous talent, it was a time of great hardship for the sensitive Irishman. Because of his recurring and very serious eye diseases, his deep blue eyes were almost hidden by thick glasses. His masterpiece, *Ulysses,* was being serialized in an American magazine, the *Little Review,* and readers of each chapter were enthralled by its startlingly beautiful use of the language, but issues of the magazine were being confiscated and even burned by officials of the United States Post Office because of the boldness of the author's language. Hopes of commercial publication of the novel were therefore diminishing, and Joyce was increasingly dependent for money on the generosity of his friends.

His friends did not fail him, and new ones changed the course of his life, among them Sylvia Beach. The two met soon after Joyce arrived in Paris; Sylvia was awed by the writer whose work she had eagerly followed and greatly admired and asked him to come to see her at Shakespeare and Company.

The following day Joyce took up her invitation; he liked the feeling of the bookshop and was immediately at home in its warmth, and he enjoyed the company of the enthusiastic Sylvia and her friend Adrienne Monnier. They, too, were charmed by Joyce: his sensitive face, with finely drawn features and little goatee; his lilting musical voice; his impeccable manners, quiet wit, and lively interest in everyone and everything around him. In their opinion the man lived up to the artist, and it was the beginning of a mutually valuable friendship.

Joyce admitted that his situation seemed a desperate one.

He needed a permanent home for his family just as he needed some work that would provide a steady income for them. Teaching English seemed the best hope.

Sylvia applied herself wholeheartedly to the task of helping, and she and Adrienne decided that it would be most useful if Joyce could become better known in French literary circles. To this end, they introduced him to Valéry Larbaud, a distinguished French writer and the most respected critic of English literature in France.

The meeting took place on Christmas Eve, 1920, at which time Larbaud was presented with copies of those chapters of *Ulysses* that had appeared in the *Little Review*. Larbaud took his time, but two months later he wrote a more than enthusiastic letter to Sylvia Beach. "I am raving mad over *Ulysses*," he said, and offered to do anything at all to help the author of this remarkable work. As a first step he planned to translate selections from the novel—an extremely difficult job—to be published together with an article on Joyce in the prestigious French literary magazine *Nouvelle Revue Française*. Before then, however, Sylvia and Adrienne thought it best to "launch" Joyce officially through a reading and discussion of his work that would be held at Adrienne's bookshop before as distinguished an audience as they could gather together.

All this was, of course, encouraging to Joyce, but the

news from America was very bad: more issues of the *Little Review* were being confiscated, and finally the two courageous woman editors of the magazine, Jane Heap and Margaret Anderson, were brought to court. After the trial, they were convicted and fined—a token fee—for publishing obscene literature. With that decision all of Joyce's hopes for commercial publication disappeared; no American or British publishing house was willing to take the risk.

It was then that Sylvia Beach acted—in a way that surprised her as much as it surprised Joyce. *She* would publish *Ulysses.* She had had absolutely no experience as a publisher, but her enormous energy and enthusiasm would make up for that lack of experience.

It was now essential for Joyce to finish his novel. He was eager to see it published in its entirety, and he wanted it completed for the Joyce evening, which Sylvia and Adrienne had decided would be for the author's financial benefit.

"Don't make a hero out of me," James Joyce once said, but he worked heroically and courageously for several months to finish *Ulysses,* often as many as seventeen hours a day. Plagued as he had been throughout his mature life with painful and serious eye trouble, which constantly threatened total blindness, there were periods during which he had to visit the eye doctor daily for treatment. There were difficult and dangerous operations, but nothing stopped his work. To read what he had written—and he could do that only with the aid of a powerful magnifying glass—he wrote every word in large letters with a large pencil on an oversized paper. Painstakingly careful, he averaged but a few hundred words a day.

While Joyce worked on his book, Sylvia Beach was busy in her new role as publisher. She arranged to have the type set and the book printed in Dijon, and busied herself in finding subscribers to the first edition, which would be limited to one thousand copies. Everyone helped: Larbaud, Adrienne, Ezra Pound, who proudly enlisted W. B. Yeats as a subscriber, Hemingway, and Robert McAlmon. The latter did more than merely solicit subscribers; he helped Joyce out financially during those difficult months and even typed some of the complicated manuscript for him.

During the summer of 1921 the first proofs of *Ulysses* began to arrive. For most authors the reading of proofs is a relatively easy job, serving largely to correct errors made by the typesetters. For the meticulous Joyce the proofs were an opportunity to rewrite his book. He carefully and painstakingly read and reread each page, adding 90,000 words to the set of proofs—almost one quarter of the book. But *Ulysses* had to be as perfect as the author could make it, and Sylvia Beach went along with each of Joyce's wishes,

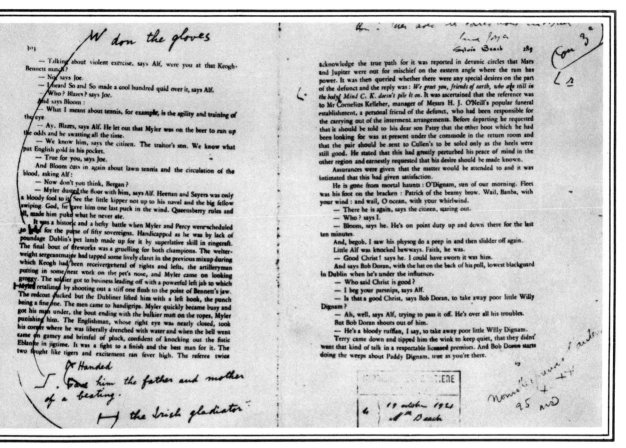

*Page proofs of* Ulysses *with editing by Joyce*

no matter what the cost to her in time and trouble.

By late fall it was time to plan Joyce's "launching" at Adrienne's bookshop. A date was decided upon, the evening of December 7. Preparations were carefully made, but as the time drew close, Larbaud began to fear that his translations wouldn't be ready. To help him out, he enlisted the aid of a young Frenchman who had a remarkable knowledge

# ULYSSES

by

# JAMES JOYCE

will be published in
the Autumn of 1921

by

"SHAKESPEARE AND COMPANY"

— *SYLVIA BEACH* —

8, RUE DUPUYTREN, PARIS — VI⁶

*Brochure announcing the publication of* Ulysses

JAMES JOYCE

*Advance Press Notices.*

— Mr. EZRA POUND in — *Instigations* — His profoundest work... an impassioned meditation on life... He has done what Flaubert set out to do in Bouvard et Pécuchet, done it better, more succint.

— Mr. RICHARD ALDINGTON in — *The English Review* — A most remarkable book... Bloom is a rags and tatters Hamlet, a proletarian Lear... An astonishing psychological document... *ULYSSES* is more bitter, more sordid, more ferociously satirical than anything Mr. JOYCE has yet written... A tremendous libel on humanity which I, at least, am not clever enough to refute.

— THE OBSERVER — ...Whatever may be thought of the work, it is going to attract almost sensational attention.

— THE TIMES — ... ... of the utmost sincerity ... complete courage.

— Mrs. EVELYN SCOTT in — *The Dial* — A contemporary of the future... His technique has developed unique aspects that indicate a revolution of style for the future... This Irish artist is recreating a portion of the English language... He uses the stuff of the whole world to prove one man.

— THE NEW AGE — ..."One of the most interesting literary symptoms in the whole literary world, and its publication is very nearly a public obligation".

— Mr. VALERY LARBAUD in — *La Nouvelle Revue Française* — Avec *ULYSSES*, l'Irlande fait une rentrée sensationnelle et triomphante dans la haute littérature européenne.

of the English language. The twenty-year-old Frenchman's only condition was that his name not be mentioned. His elderly father, a baron, would not approve of his son's connection with the notorious *Ulysses*.

It was indeed a daring novel, even for France. While telling of one day in the life of two Dubliners—Stephen Dedalus and Leopold Bloom—Joyce had written vividly, employing utterly frank language and descriptions of sexual acts that had never before seen print. The book, with its detailed rendering of Dublin life, displayed an unprecedented virtuosity of style as well as an eccentricity of form. It therefore puzzled many readers, but it bore the unmistakable mark of genius.

*Ulysses* had been banned and feared for what might be considered "offensive" language, and even before a group of selected and interested intellectuals that night in Paris, explanations—if not apologies—seemed necessary. On the program Larbaud put the following warning: "We warn the public that certain pages that will be read are of an unusual boldness which might, legitimately, be offensive." The French critic, in spite of his vast experience as a lecturer, had to have his courage bolstered before the reading by a glass of brandy, and even with the brandy he deleted a small part of Joyce's text.

But the lecture went well, and the audience of two hundred and fifty people who jammed the room were fascinated as Valéry Larbaud read selections of Joyce, gave a biographical summary of the Irishman's life, and a critical talk on his writing. When he finished, Adrienne Monnier introduced the American actor Jimmy Light, who would read some of *Ulysses* in English. She, too, however, felt it necessary to warn the audience of the "audacious" language they would be hearing.

She need not have feared, for when the evening came to an end there was a burst of wild applause, which only increased when Larbaud found Joyce, shyly hiding behind a screen, and forced him to come out and face the cheering audience. Larbaud embraced the blushing Irishman, kissing him on both cheeks, as the French do. The evening had been a complete triumph.

Two months later, on Joyce's fortieth birthday, February 2, 1922, the first copies of *Ulysses* were ready. Literary history had been made in Paris. Shortly afterward, James Joyce began work on his next book, *Finnegans Wake*, which would take him seventeen years to complete.

# 8

# A Kind of Summit Meeting

Just as James Joyce was the dominant literary figure in Paris during the twenties, Igor Stravinsky, a Russian, was the major figure in the world of music. Both of these men were innovators to whom the expatriates looked up.

Unlike Joyce, Stravinsky was no longer struggling for recognition and financial success during the twenties; he had already firmly established himself as a composer of rare originality and genius in the years preceding the First World War, largely through his scores for Sergei Diaghilev's world-renowned Russian Ballet. It was his association with this fabled ballet company that led to one of the most glamorous parties of the decade, a dinner on the river Seine given by Sara and Gerald Murphy, two most unusual American expatriates.

*Portrait of Igor Stravinsky by Picasso*

Stravinsky was born in a suburb of Saint Petersburg in 1882—the same year that Joyce was born near Dublin. The son of a well-known opera singer, he showed a precocious interest in and talent for music from his earliest years. While at school, he made up his mind to be a composer, and he never wavered from this ambition.

By 1908 his early compositions had already come to the attention of Diaghilev, an intellectual of many and varied talents, who was organizing a Paris season for his new company, the Russian Ballet, which would take place during the summer of 1909. The twenty-six-year-old Stravinsky was asked to orchestrate some of Chopin's piano music for the new ballet *Les Sylphides.* Diaghilev was so impressed with Stravinsky's work that he commissioned him to write the music for a major new ballet to be performed in Paris the next season, *The Firebird,* based on a Russian folktale and choreographed by Michel Fokine.

The premiere of *The Firebird* took place on June 25, 1910. The audience, which included three of the world's leading composers—Manuel de Falla, Claude Debussy, and Maurice Ravel—was dazzled by the brilliant score that Stravinsky had composed; the young Russian became famous overnight.

The following year came another success—*Petrouchka*—and in 1913 Diaghilev produced Stravinsky's *The Rite of Spring,* with choreography by Nijinsky. The audience was jolted by Stravinsky's dynamic and powerful rhythms, and the first-night performance was the occasion for rioting and fighting in the audience—between champions and oppo-

*Sergei Diaghilev and Salisburg, his manager*

nents of the work—such as rarely has occurred in a theatre. It was not long, however, before *The Rite of Spring* was universally recognized as the masterpiece that it is.

By the end of World War One, when he returned to

Paris in 1920, Stravinsky's music had been played all over the world. The Russian Ballet, too, had achieved world-wide fame and attracted immense crowds in whatever city it performed. Sergei Diaghilev had done something for the ballet that had never been done before. To complement his brilliant assemblage of dancers and choreographers, among them Nijinsky, Pavlova, Fokine, Massine, Lifar, and Balanchine—all of them still spoken of today—he had recruited the greatest artists to design the productions and the finest composers to write the music to accompany the ballets. The painters included Picasso, Juan Gris, Georges Braque, Maurice Utrillo, and André Derain. Among the composers were Debussy, Ravel, de Falla, Milhaud, Satie, Prokofiev, and, of course, Stravinsky himself. Never before —or since—has such a distinguished group of creators in diverse fields collaborated in the world of ballet.

The highlight of the Russian Ballet's 1923 season in Paris (they never performed in Russia!) was to be a new work by Stravinsky, and its premiere was eagerly anticipated. Its title was *The Wedding* (often known by its French title, *Les Noces*); the composer had started work on it in 1914, finished it in 1917, and was completing the definitive instrumentation in 1923.

Present at every rehearsal of *The Wedding* were a handsome, elegant, and charming couple, Sara and Gerald

Murphy. The Murphys were American expatriates, but they had little in common with those Americans who spent their days sleeping and their nights sitting at cafés along the boulevard Montparnasse; nor had they much in common with those more serious expatriates who lived on severely limited incomes and devoted themselves to their growth as creative artists.

For the Murphys were wealthy—they had a substantial private income that went a long way in Paris at the time; and they had three children and lived a more regulated family life as a result. They had come to Europe not to seek new ways of self-expression, but in search of a more congenial and gracious way of living than they could find in America.

As soon as the Murphys arrived in Paris, they threw themselves energetically into the city's cultural activities. Though they became good friends of Hemingway and Mac-Leish and, most notably, Scott Fitzgerald, their interest was largely in the visual arts, and they soon became friends of the many painters of all nationalities who were working in Paris. They were most enthusiastic, too, about the Russian Ballet. "In addition to being the focal center of the whole modern movement in the arts," Murphy is quoted as saying by Calvin Tomkins, "the Diaghilev ballet was a kind of movement in itself. Anyone who was interested in the

*Igor Stravinsky and Leonide Massine*

company became a member automatically. You knew everybody, you knew all the dancers, and everybody asked your opinion on things."

The Murphys had been "members" since their early days in Paris, when they had both volunteered to help repaint Diaghilev sets to replace those that had been destroyed by a warehouse fire. It was largely through their connection with the Russian impresario that they became friends with those Frenchmen—and foreigners—who were usually outside American expatriate circles. They were on excellent terms with Stravinsky who once said, "The Murphys were among the first Americans I ever met, and they gave me the most agreeable impression of the United States." Both Murphys, too, had studied painting with Natalia Goncharova, who was designing the curtain, costumes, and scenery for *The Wedding.*

As they watched rehearsals for this new ballet, the Murphys realized that its premiere should be a cause for celebration. They would do their part by giving a party— and their parties were famous for their elegance and taste— to honor those who had participated in the creation of *The Wedding.*

Their expectations for the success of the ballet were more than borne out by the enthusiastic reception given to this stunning new work at its opening on June 13, 1923. The

*The Wedding*

gala audience that packed the Théâtre de la Gaîté Lyrique
that spring night was delighted with each aspect of the production. Goncharova's sets for this ballet—which depicted
through four tableaux the preparation for a Russian village
wedding—consisted of simple mystical black and white
backcloths; Bronislava Nijinska's choreography was noble,

more like "cubistic plastic posing" than dance, according to Janet Flanner, and most effective. And Stravinsky's score for this choral ballet was lyrical and strikingly original. Instead of a full orchestra, he employed singers, four pianos, and a large group of percussion instruments—timbals, bells, and xylophones—to contrast with the lyricism of the vocal parts. The work was conducted by the Swiss conductor Ernest Ansermet, the outstanding interpreter of Stravinsky's music, and three prominent contemporary composers had agreed to play the piano parts: Francis Poulenc, Vittorio Rieti, and Georges Auric. (The fourth piano part was played by Marcelle Mayer, known for her performances of modern music.) It was, in every way, a gala occasion and a night to remember.

Four nights later, on Sunday June 17, the Murphys gave their party, and in its way it was an equally gala occasion.

After looking around for a suitable location for this very special party, the Murphys decided on a restaurant that had been built on a barge on the Seine, in front of the Chambre des Députés. On every night except Sunday, it was for the exclusive use of the French representatives, but since the party was to be held on a Sunday, the barge was made available for the occasion.

The guest list, as Calvin Tomkins wrote, "constituted a kind of summit meeting of the modern movement in Paris."

Among the painters were Picasso, Goncharova and her husband Michel Larionov. The musicians included Ansermet and Darius Milhaud. From the world of literature there were Jean Cocteau; Blaise Cendrars, the poet; Tristan Tzara, the father of Dada, then *the* most discussed artistic movement in Paris; and Scofield Thayer, editor of the *Dial*, an American literary magazine. Of course, Diaghilev himself attended, as did four or five female dancers and two male principals from the company.

The first guest to arrive for the party, which was to start at seven o'clock, was Stravinsky who went immediately to the dining room to arrange the place cards the way he wanted them. Appropriately, he saw that he was seated next to the Princess Edmond de Polignac, an American of the Singer sewing machine family, who had commissioned *The Wedding* and was known for the salons held in her magnificent home on the chic avenue Henri-Martin where first performances of works by Ravel, Debussy, Satie—and *The Wedding*—had been heard.

Before the dinner itself, cocktails were served on the upper deck of the refurbished barge, after which the guests descended to the dining room. There they found a long banquet table decorated with little pyramids of gaily colored, fanciful toys, which ran down the length of the table. The Murphys had been unable to find fresh flowers on a

Sunday, and the idea of substituting them with toys had been an unexpected—and delightful—inspiration, which the guests found charming. Picasso was particularly pleased; he gathered up several of them and combined them into an improvised "work of art," with a cow on a fireman's ladder on the top.

The magnificent champagne dinner lasted for several hours; at intervals between courses there was music by Ansermet and Marcelle Mayer who played the piano at one end of the room, and there was dancing by members of the company. Cocteau came late—he was terrified of seasickness and refused to join the group until there was no danger of a passing riverboat that could rock the barge. But his entrance was a dramatic one: dressed in the barge captain's uniform, he carried a lantern as he went from porthole to porthole announcing that the barge was sinking.

Hanging from the dining room's ceiling was a huge laurel wreath with the inscription "*Les Noces—Hommages.*" To the Murphys' surprise, Ansermet and Diaghilev's secretary took it down and held it for Stravinsky who ran across the room and through the wreath.

As Tomkins has written: "No one really got drunk, no one went home much before dawn, and no one, in all probability, has ever forgotten the party."

# 9

# *Everyone Knew They Had Been Somewhere*

Among the audience at the premiere of *The Wedding* were the twenty-two-year-old musician George Antheil and his young Hungarian friend Boski. It was their first day in Paris, where they had come to live from Germany; they were guests of the great Stravinsky who had befriended Antheil in Berlin, and they were dressed for the occasion. "Boski's Berlin gown was a black velvet tight-fitting low-cut affair, setting off her jet-black hair and that brown-blue glint which all Hungarians seem to flash from their otherwise white epidermis," Antheil wrote in his memoirs. "I personally looked ridiculous. I was dressed in an expensive full-dress suit which Hanson had specially tailored for me in London. I also wore a soft hat and a *cape of my own*

*George Antheil*

*design* tailored by the same Berlin tailor who had made my silken padded revolver holster for my left armpit."

Antheil carried a revolver for a good reason, for the ultramodern music he played at his concerts seemed to provoke riots among stunned audiences. The moment the audience began to stir, the young American would calmly remove the revolver from under his arm and place it on the piano. He was taking no chances. The bold, publicity-conscious young man had come to Europe for the same reasons that so many American composers and musicians—among them Aaron Copland, Roy Harris, and Virgil Thomson—had. "Musically, it is impossible to live in America. A young composer has absolutely no future in America, because, even if he attains the very peak of eminence, he cannot hope to make a livelihood, whereas in Europe he stands a chance of making anywhere from a decent livelihood to even the accumulation of a fortune," he wrote. If Antheil didn't accumulate a fortune, he most certainly made a name for himself during his Paris years. His uncanny ability to meet the right people never failed him.

His luck started when he went searching for an apartment and found a small one at 12 rue de l'Odéon, above Shakespeare and Company. Sylvia Beach felt an immediate bond between them, Antheil's father having been the owner of the Friendly Shoestore in Trenton, New Jersey, not far from Princeton. She was also interested in the young man's musical ideas and taken with his boyish charm. With his angelic face and straight bangs, he looked to her like an American high-school boy.

Before long, the cheerful, self-confident young man came to know the most prominent literary expatriates in Paris, most of whom were won over by his big grin and lively in-

*Virgil Thomson*

telligence. One who was not wholly won over was Robert McAlmon who helped him financially but had reservations: "I must confess," he wrote, "that George struck me a bit too deliberately boyish, naïve, and ingenuous, for the lad never neglected to cultivate, in his naïve-est manner, whoever might serve his ends."

Antheil did make the right friends, among them Jean Cocteau, James Joyce and, above all, Ezra Pound. The red-bearded poet prided himself on discovering genius and promoting it, and Antheil became his discovery. He even wrote a short book about the young composer, *Antheil and the Treatise on Harmony*, for which Antheil was not very grateful. "Ezra's flamboyant book," he wrote, "couched in language calculated to antagonize everyone first by its ridiculous praise, then by its vicious criticism of everybody else, did me no good whatsoever; on the contrary, it sowed the most active distaste for the very mention of the name 'Antheil' among contemporary critics, prejudiced them before they had even so much as heard a note of mine."

Whatever Antheil thought of the book, it did establish him as a "name," and this notoriety undoubtedly led to his being asked to play a concert at Paris's elegant Théâtre des Champs-Elysées. It was not exactly *his* evening—his performance was to be a prelude to the opening of the famous Swedish Ballet—but it was a chance not to be missed.

*George Antheil climbing to his apartment above Shakespeare and Company*

All Paris was there, the night of October 4, 1923, including the greatest names of the time: Picasso, Stravinsky, Joyce, Satie, Man Ray, Diaghilev, Miró, Ford Madox Ford, and Artur Rubinstein. They had come to see the renowned ballet company, but they would also hear George Antheil play his controversial, riot-provoking compositions. They were not disappointed. A few moments after Antheil started playing his group of piano pieces, the rioting began. The musician felt the audience stir and he instinctively reached for his ever-present pistol. There was fighting, shouting, and total chaos, which didn't die out until the end of the performance.

From the moment he came on stage, Antheil had realized that the stage floodlights were particularly strong. Later they were turned on the audience, even directly in Joyce's face, damaging his sensitive eyes. A year later Antheil learned the reason. The riot, though genuine, had been part of a plot, and the strong lighting was essential to it, for a movie was to be made featuring a riot, and those who were making the film rightly predicted that they would be able to film a real one at an Antheil concert.

The next Antheil "riot" was not filmed, but many of those present have written colorful accounts of it. It was over what has remained Antheil's most famous work, the

*Ballet Méchanique.* He had worked on this experimental piece of music for a few years; it had been used as part of a film and had been privately performed. Because of this, all Paris was talking about it and eagerly awaiting the premiere, which took place on Saturday night, June 19, 1926.

The setting was once again the enormous Théâtre des Champs-Elysées, and an immense crowd pushed their way into the auditorium. Excitement was in the air, a feeling that *something* was going to happen at the performance of this much-heralded work. It was an interesting group— Joyce, Pound, and even T. S. Eliot, who was rarely seen in public—and the American journalist Lincoln Steffens noted "all the queer people in Paris, French and foreign, men and women. Wild hair, flannel shirts, sticks, no hats and big hats for both men and women, and, note well, many intelligent faces."

The crowd rushed to find their seats, but they needn't have hurried. The star attraction—Antheil—had discovered a moth hole in the front of his tails that had to be sewn before he could go on stage, so the concert was somewhat delayed.

The evening began calmly, with the conductor Vladimir Golschmann leading the orchestra in a performance of the overture to *Der Freischütz*, which was followed by a Handel *Concerto Grosso*. Then came an Antheil *Symphony in F*, a noncontroversial work to which no one in the audience would object.

But then it was time for the *Ballet Méchanique*. This was sure to be different; and it was.

In the center of the stage stood a huge airplane propeller. Around it were eight regular pianos and one mechanical player piano which, at Antheil's command, controlled a number of xylophones, electric bells, whistles, and loudspeakers. As soon as the performance began, the audience began to stir. Based on his previous experiences, Antheil knew what to expect. These sounds were, the composer explained, "all part of the musical sounds of our modern life," but the noisy pianos, loud whistles, and clanging bells jolted and angered much of the public. Catcalls and booing and loud shouting competed with roars of approval and cries of bravo. The music was loud, but not as loud as the audience response. Soon, the aisles were jammed with people—trying to get to the musicians or just trying to leave.

In the midst of all this confusion the airplane propeller began to turn, blowing strong gusts of cold wind throughout the theatre. People turned up their coat collars or raised their umbrellas as a protection against the icy blasts. It was reported that one distinguished listener's wig was blown off by the force of the wind and found its way to the back of the theatre.

The wind fanned an even greater fury, and members of the elegantly dressed audience started lashing out at each other with walking sticks and umbrellas and throwing aimless punches in all directions.

Forgotten in all this and largely unheard—because of the noise—was the *Ballet Méchanique,* but when the concert came to a close, there was a wild ovation for George Antheil. It was an audience that cared about music—strongly enough to attack it or defend it. "There was an atmosphere about the theatre most wholesome for the art of music," the Paris *Tribune* reported the following day. "Everyone knew they had been somewhere."

It is safe to say that no one who had been there forgot this violent premiere, nor could anyone have forgotten the one voice that outshouted all others in crying "Silence, imbeciles"—the voice of Ezra Pound.

# 10

# *That Bearded Adventurer Who Dealt in Masterpieces*

The voice of Ezra Pound, the high-strung, opinionated, and brilliant American poet with the pointed beard and the wild shock of carrot-colored hair, was often heard above all others as he passionately promoted those causes most dear to him. There were worthy ones, such as his selfless dedication to some of the greatest writers of this century; and there were disgraceful ones, such as the fascism and anti-Semitism he espoused before and during World War Two.

The seeds of his distasteful political and social views had undoubtedly been planted before he came to Paris, but his few years in the French capital are noteworthy for his tireless energy and enthusiasm in promoting what he felt was the best in current literature. The Ezra Pound of those

*Ezra Pound*

years was indeed "that bearded adventurer who dealt in masterpieces," as Charles Norman describes him.

He was born in Hailey, Idaho, on October 30, 1885. At the age of fifteen he entered the University of Pennsylvania and then went on to Hamilton College, from which he received his degree; he later returned to Pennsylvania where he did graduate work in romance languages. His interest in languages had been intense, and his plan when he entered college was to study eight or nine of them. Love of languages, too, led to his early interest in poetry, and while at college he conducted poetic experiments with his medical school friend, William Carlos Williams, also destined to become a major poet.

Pound was a restless and nervous young man, ever seeking change, and after teaching French and Spanish at Wabash College in Indiana for four months in 1908—he was expelled from the college for keeping a girl in his room overnight—he decided to sail for Europe. He traveled about the Continent, settled for a while in Venice where his first book of poetry, *A lume spento,* was published (at his own expense), and then moved to London.

In London he found a job teaching medieval romance literature, while pursuing his own career as a writer and critic. Before long, the young man became a part of the literary life of the capital, counting among his friends

William Butler Yeats, for whom he served as secretary for three winters, and Ford Madox Ford, the influential English writer and editor. Young Pound led a movement called Imagism, the roots of which were in medieval philosophy, Japanese poetry, and the works of Henri Bergson, and edited the first collection of imagist poetry, *Some Imagist Poets,* which included his own works as well as short poems —by William Carlos Williams, Hilda Doolittle, and Richard Aldington—all of which adhered to the imagist theory of absolute precision and musical cadences in poetry.

During those London years, too, Pound became associated with three little magazines: he was literary editor of the *Egoist,* a British publication; London editor of the *Little Review,* an American magazine; and foreign correspondent for *Poetry: a Magazine of Verse,* edited in Chicago. In these roles he not only found publishers for his own poetry but was able to advocate the work of writers he felt to be deserving of publication.

By 1920 he was a powerful figure on the British literary scene, but he had tired of London and was increasingly irritated by the squabbles among British writers. He found the "decay of the British Empire too depressing a spectacle to witness at close range." He briefly thought of returning to the United States, but decided to go to Paris, the "one live spot in Europe," to look for "a poetic serum to save

English literature from postmature and American literature from premature suicide and decomposition."

At first, he found the French capital to be a refreshing change from the physical and mental climate he had hated in London, and in no time he became a familiar figure on Paris's Left Bank. Over six feet tall, but somewhat clumsy, he was often seen hurrying along the streets, a flopping wide hat on his head, his beard pointed forward, his slender frame followed by a long cloak that trailed behind him. He always seemed distracted, his mind always active in the pursuit of new ideas or projects. Often he carried a walking stick and occasionally he stopped in a café, not for a leisurely drink but to keep an appointment, and it was not unusual for him to leave without a goodbye when his mission had been accomplished.

During his Paris years he worked hard on what was to be his lifetime masterpiece, the *Cantos,* but he had more than enough time for "causes." In addition to promoting the musical career of George Antheil, he "adopted" Constantin Brancusi, the innovative Rumanian sculptor, just as he had given his all to another sculptor, Gaudier-Brzeska, in the years before World War One. While translating works by Jean Cocteau and Rémy de Gourmont, he found time to discover writers of promise and bring them to the attention of the magazines he represented, now in-

cluding *The Dial,* for which he contributed a "Paris letter."

His home in Paris, for which he paid thirty dollars a
month, was a crowded studio at 70 bis rue Notre Dame des
Champs, not far from the boulevard Montparnasse. It was
on the ground floor, off a courtyard, overlooking a garden.

The large room told much about the man who lived in
it. It looked as much like an art gallery as it did a home;
paintings hung two and three deep from the walls, many
of them by Pound's Japanese artist friends, and odds and
ends of sculpture were scattered throughout. The poet liked
to make his own furniture, and prominent in the room was
a low scarlet-colored tea table made from old packing cases,
as well as two large armchairs that had been put together
out of rough boards and canvas. In one corner of the room
were his University of Pennsylvania fencing foils, and any
available space was covered with overstuffed bookshelves,
revealing Pound's astoundingly wide range of literary interests.

It was in this setting that Ezra Pound played host—as
well as editor and critic—to a remarkable assemblage of
writers and artists. "He helped poets, painters, sculptors
and prose writers that he believed in," wrote Ernest Hemingway, "and he would help anyone whether he believed
in them or not if they were in trouble."

Hemingway spoke from his own experience with Pound, who was as important to him as was Gertrude Stein. He had come to the poet's studio in 1922 and, though at first he found Pound to be pretentiously Bohemian, the two soon became friends. Pound read some of Hemingway's poems and stories and liked them. He edited the young American's work with sensitivity and intelligence, helping Hemingway develop that style that was to be characterized by a severe economy of words. Believing that his stories represented something new in American literature, he tried to place Hemingway's work in the magazines with which he was connected.

In return, the burly athletic Hemingway gave Pound boxing lessons. "He's teaching me to write, and I'm teaching him to box," he told a friend. Pound was never much of a boxer—he had neither the strength nor the temperament. But Hemingway, of course, became a writer, and much of his early success was due to Pound's unselfish help.

It was through Pound that Hemingway had his first chance at book publication, when the former included a collection of the young writer's work in a series of small volumes to be printed and published, under Pound's direction, by a small expatriate publishing house on Paris's Ile-St.-Louis called Three Mountains Press. And he later

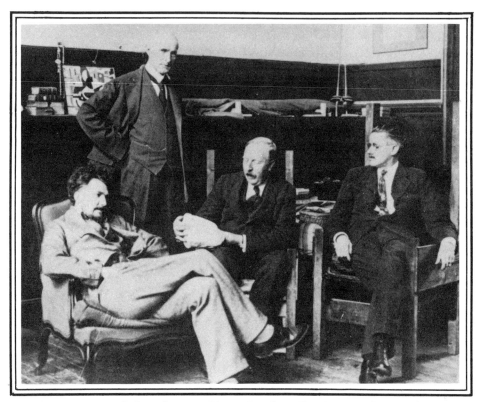

*Ezra Pound, John Quinn, Ford Madox Ford, and James Joyce*

convinced Ford Madox Ford to take Hemingway on as his assistant editor for Ford's *Transatlantic Review*. "Ezra was," Hemingway said, "the most generous writer I have ever known and the most disinterested."

James Joyce, too, was among those to whom Pound gave wholehearted and unselfish encouragement, saying later in his life that "it is probable that but for him I should still be the unknown drudge that he discovered." Pound first heard of the great Irish writer from Yeats in 1913. He wrote to Joyce, telling him of his connection with *Poetry, Egoist,* and other magazines, and asking him to send him some of his writing. Joyce did so at once, and Pound responded enthusiastically. It was, to him, "great stuff," and he did something about it. First, he saw to it that the *Egoist* began to serialize *A Portrait of the Artist as a Young Man;* then he struggled to have it published as a book. Next, he convinced Margaret Anderson and Jane Heap of the *Little Review* to publish excerpts from *Ulysses,* a decision that caused the magazine to be banned and burned but always remembered for its taste and discernment.

Pound also did what he could to help Joyce solve his often desperate personal problems. He felt it was a crime that a great writer should be almost penniless and tried to find money for the Irish writer wherever he could. Occasionally, he succeeded, as in the case of his attempts to get a grant for Joyce from the Royal Literary Fund, which helped Joyce survive for a while. It was Pound who sensed that Joyce would be happiest in Paris, and it was he who showed him the way when he arrived there. "I owe a great deal to his friendly help, encouragement and generous interest in everything I have written," Joyce stated. "He helped me in every possible way in the face of very great difficulties for seven years before I met him, and since then he has always been ready to give me advice and ap-

*T. S. Eliot*

preciation which I esteem very highly as coming from a mind of such brilliance and discernment."

Another major writer who benefited greatly from Pound's friendship was T. S. Eliot. Pound met the American-born poet in London in 1914, encouraged him to settle in England and, impressed with his talent, set about trying to find a publisher for his poetry. However, no writer could live on his earnings as a poet, and Eliot was forced to spend most of his time working in a London bank in order to subsist. Pound tried to find a solution. He himself had been helped by the American lawyer John Quinn, a friend and patron to a huge number of artists and writers during the first part of this century, and on June 4, 1920, he wrote to Quinn of Eliot's plight.

"No use blinking the fact that it is a crime against literature to let him waste eight hours vitality per diem in that bank." He had a practical suggestion as well—that Eliot be subsidized anonymously. "Is there any bloody chance," he asked Quinn, "of raising this sum from four or five people who would keep their mouths shut?" To show his earnestness he himself offered to give Eliot fifty pounds a year for three years at great personal sacrifice. Quinn, too, offered to contribute fifty pounds a year, but he refused to solicit help from others, and the idea had to be temporarily dropped.

Before a similar scheme was proposed by Pound, he had a chance to help Eliot in another way—an even more important one. Eliot's health had been poor; he had suffered a nervous collapse from which he had only just recovered when he came to Paris in late 1921 to show Pound a copy of the manuscript of his latest poem, *The Waste Land*. "I placed before him in Paris the manuscript of a sprawling, chaotic poem called *The Waste Land*," Eliot recalled later, "which left his hands, reduced to about half its size, in the form in which it appears in print." Pound considered the poem to be a masterpiece, and he applied all his creative energy to help Eliot improve it. Rarely has one poet helped another so intelligently, and Eliot was forever grateful. "I should like to think," he wrote, "that the manuscript, with the suppressed passages, had disappeared irrecoverably; yet, on the other hand, I should wish the blue pencilling on it to be irrefutable proof of Pound's critical genius."

If Pound was more than ever convinced that Eliot was one of the major writers of his time, he was also more than ever concerned with the latter's health, which was again failing, and the fact that he still had to lose eight hours a day working in a bank. He thus revived his old scheme for providing Eliot with a steady and secure income, a scheme he later hoped to apply to other worthy writers who for economic reasons were unable to devote their full energies to their writing. This time his plan had a name, "Bel Esprit," and it called for thirty people to contribute ten pounds (about fifty dollars) a year to support a needy author—for life or for as long as necessary. Eliot, of course, was to be the first recipient of this grant, and Pound typed up his ideas, sending around carbon copies to possible participants in the plan, explaining that Eliot had written "one of the most important 19 pages in English."

A few weeks later he sent out printed leaflets, praising *The Waste Land* as "a series of poems, possibly the finest that the modern movement in English has produced, at any rate as good as anything that has been done since 1900, and which certainly lose nothing by comparison with the best work of Keats, Browning or Shelley." The leaflet explained that Eliot's work at the bank was exhausting and left him too little energy for his writing. There was also the announcement that the initial lifetime subscribers included Richard Aldington and May Sinclair, two distinguished British writers, as well as Pound himself.

Unfortunately, the well-intentioned plan became a source of embarrassment to Eliot. "I think you will agree that the method proposed by Ezra is rather bordering on the precarious and slightly undignified charity. At the bank I am at least independent of the people whom I know, and a doubtful income, which I should be obliged to attempt to double by literary work would not be the slightest advantage from anyone's point of view," the poet wrote to Aldington. Later, as the result of an inaccurate account of the plan that was published in the Liverpool *Post,* Eliot was further embarrassed. Anonymous gifts began to arrive, one donor sending him four postage stamps. Eliot's family, too, heard of the plan in America and were enraged by the idea of their son taking what amounted to charity.

Pound was stubborn, however, and went ahead, but Eliot absolutely refused to take any money, and "Bel Esprit" finally collapsed. Only years later did Pound admit that the whole idea had been "a dismal nervewracking failure for everyone concerned."

By 1924 Ezra Pound had tired of Paris, much as he had of London. He felt put upon by the expatriate literary colony and was uncomfortable among them. He also believed that more important things were happening elsewhere in Europe—there was no thought of returning to the United States—and was sure he would be happier in Italy, where he was to spend most of the rest of his life.

Nonetheless, he had led a good life in Paris and could have no regrets: it would always be remembered as one of his most productive and least controversial periods. As if to commemorate Pound's Parisian stay, the first issue of

*Painting of Ernest Walsh by Ethel Moorhead*

a new magazine, published in 1925, was dedicated to him.

It was called *This Quarter* and was edited by a brilliant but frail and consumptive Irish-American writer named Ernest Walsh and his, as well as the magazine's, benefactor Ethel Moorhead, a fearless and determined Scottish heiress who spent much of her money in the cause of the arts. The dedication of this excellent magazine was to Ezra Pound, "who by his creative work, his editorship of several magazines, his helpful friendship for young and unknown artists, his many and untiring efforts to win better appreciation of what is first-rate in art comes first to our mind as meriting the gratitude of this generation."

There were effusive tributes by Walsh and Moorhead as well as by Joyce and Hemingway. The latter wrote:

So far, we have Pound the major poet devoting, say, one fifth of his time to poetry. With the rest of his time he tries to advance the fortunes, both material and artistic, of his friends. He defends them when they are attacked, he gets them into magazines and out of jail. He loans them money. He sells their pictures. He arranges concerts for them. He writes articles about them. He introduces them to wealthy women. He gets publishers to take their books. He sits up all night with them when they claim to be dying and he witnesses their wills. He advances them hospital expenses and dissuades them from suicide.

This first issue of an exciting new magazine was a fitting

tribute to Pound, yet somehow things soured within a short time between the poet and Ethel Moorhead. Ernest Walsh died tragically at the age of thirty-one, and—because Moorhead felt he had not been sufficiently helped by Pound who himself seems to have been offended because his editorial suggestions for the magazine were not followed—the owner of *This Quarter,* in its third issue, bitterly withdrew the earlier dedication.

Many people, but for far different reasons, were to retract dedications of many kinds that they had made to Ezra Pound during his lifetime. As for his years in Paris, and his decision to leave there, the words of Ernest Hemingway provide the best summary:

Like all men who become famous very young he suffers from not being read. It is so much easier to talk about a classic than to read it. There is another generation, though, in America that is replacing the generation that decided Ezra could not be a great poet because he was actually alive and kicking, and this generation is reading him. They come to Paris and want to meet him. But he has gone to Italy.

As he takes no interest in Italian politics and does not mind Italian cookery he may stay there some time. It is good for him to be there because his friends cannot get at him so easily and energy is thus released for production.

Pound stayed in Italy, but, unfortunately, he did take an interest in the disastrous Italian politics of the period.

This led to his angry pro-fascist and anti-American views that he expressed throughout World War Two, and has led to his position as a highly controversial figure in the history of American literature. He is now, with good reason, a much-hated symbol, but his eminence and positive influence in the literary world of Paris in the twenties and his unselfish devotion to the cause of his fellow artists can never be denied.

# 11

# *A Proving Ground for the New Literature*

A good deal of Ezra Pound's work was published in, and his energies channeled through, the so-called little magazines, the names of which fill the pages of every story of the expatriate Americans in Paris during the twenties. They were called "little" because they appealed to a small select audience and thus had a limited circulation. "Little," too, might have been applied to the amount of money these magazines had to sustain themselves, and to the amount of money they could afford to pay to their contributors—even the richest of the magazines rarely paid more than a dollar a page.

Their influence, however, was enormous, for it was in these small courageous publications that most (a study of

these magazines reveals the figure to be about 80 percent)
of the important writers of this century first saw their works
in print.

As opposed to the widely read commercial magazines
that were unwilling to try something new, these journals
prided themselves on their willingness to experiment; they
encouraged that innovation that leads to true art. It was
literary quality that counted; the editors of the little magazines didn't care if an author was known or unknown, if
his or her work was difficult or easy to understand. They
didn't try to become popular, scorning large circulation
because they were not dependent on advertisers. Because
they printed works that were often incomprehensible to
most readers, they were sometimes made fun of, but while
those mass-circulation popular magazines of the first part
of this century are now largely forgotten, the little magazines have retained an important place in the history of
American literature. They provided a forum for Hemingway, Joyce, and Stein, among countless others, who were
unable to have their writings published elsewhere.

There were many of these magazines, most of them based
in Europe and the majority of them published in Paris.
Ezra Pound himself published *Exile* in 1927 and 1928,
and there were *Gargoyle, Broom* (printed in Rome), *Seces-
sion,* and, of course, *This Quarter.* To a different degree

each made a valid contribution in publishing writers of the avant-garde.

Three magazines, however, were of major importance. One was the *Little Review,* the magazine that first dared to publish excerpts from *Ulysses.* It had been founded in Chicago by a beautiful and courageous woman named Margaret Anderson in 1914, and before Anderson and her assistant Jane Heap moved themselves and their magazine to Paris, they had worked from both San Francisco and New York. In a sense, the *Little Review's* transferral to Paris was a return home, for the authors whose works it printed—Stein, Pound, Joyce, and Hemingway—were living in the French capital at that time.

Margaret Anderson's greatest gift to the magazine was her enthusiasm. Her aim, she stated, was "to print the best conversations the world has to offer," and her wisest move was to appoint Ezra Pound as her foreign editor. Anderson's zest and energy combined with Pound's taste in finding new talent made many issues of the *Little Review* memorable, but lack of capital proved to be its downfall. Starting as a monthly magazine, it became a quarterly in 1922, and by 1929 it was forced to stop publication.

Another daring magazine, but one that lasted for only thirteen issues, was *Transatlantic Review,* edited by Ford Madox Ford. A stout man with a pink complexion and a

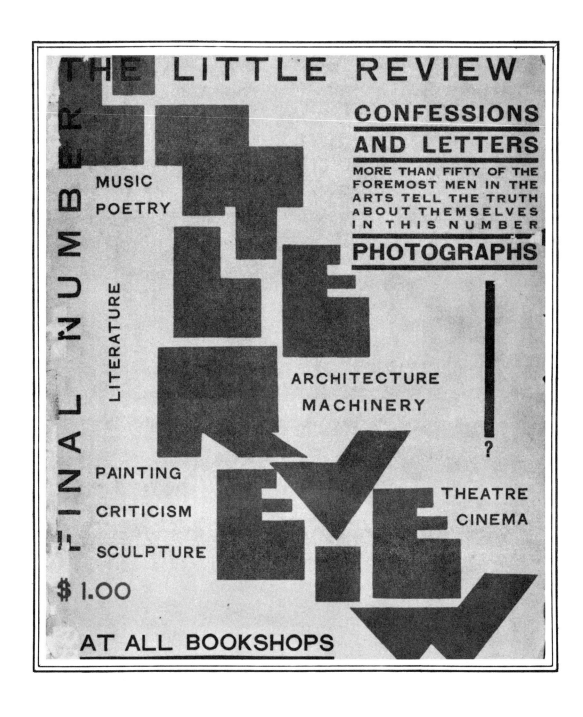

# THE LITTLE REVIEW

FINAL NUMBER

MUSIC
POETRY

LITERATURE

PAINTING

CRITICISM

SCULPTURE

$ 1.00

CONFESSIONS
AND LETTERS

MORE THAN FIFTY OF THE
FOREMOST MEN IN THE
ARTS TELL THE TRUTH
ABOUT THEMSELVES
IN THIS NUMBER

PHOTOGRAPHS

ARCHITECTURE
MACHINERY

?

THEATRE
CINEMA

AT ALL BOOKSHOPS

tobacco-stained walrus moustache, Ford was considerably older and more conservative than most of the men and women who surrounded him. An Englishman, he had been a friend and collaborator of Joseph Conrad, had written several novels, including *The Good Soldier,* and had founded a successful magazine in London, the *English Review*. Already successful, he was sure of his own talent and taste.

The first issue of *Transatlantic Review,* published from a small office on the Ile-St.-Louis, was dated January 1924. It included poetry by Pound and e. e. cummings, and later issues included works by Joyce, Dos Passos, William Carlos Williams, Djuna Barnes, Robert McAlmon, and Hemingway. It was when the latter, at Pound's recommendation, came to *Transatlantic Review* as assistant editor that the direction of the magazine changed its course. Money was short, and John Quinn, Ford's original backer, died in New York, so the Englishman was forced to spend more time in raising money for the magazine than in editing it. Soon it reflected Hemingway's taste—particularly in the publication of midwestern American writers—more than it did Ford's. Ford greatly admired these American writers, but did not feel they should be published instead of his own special favorites. The imprint of his own personality was not being felt in the magazine. Though Ford

*Ford Madox Ford*

gave his young American editor great latitude, bitter quarrels between the two men ensued and *Transatlantic Review* suspended publication in 1925.

All these magazines, in the sense that they published works that broke with tradition and defied the forces of conservatism, were revolutionary; but the most revolutionary of them all—and also the most enduring—was one called *transition*.

Largely responsible for this magazine's success was a fascinating man named Eugene Jolas. Though in the early years he had the valuable aid of Elliot Paul as copublisher and editor, it was Jolas's spirit and temperament that left the greatest mark on the magazine. His background was an unusual one and played a considerable part in the direction his magazine was to take. It is compassionately and intelligently described by his widow, Maria Jolas, in *A James Joyce Miscellany*, published by the James Joyce Society in 1957.

Eugene Jolas was the eldest of eight children of poor, devoutly Catholic parents who lived in a little town on the Franco-German frontier. Although he was actually born in the United States, his parents' return to Europe when he was two years old made him linguistically and intellectually a European, as he only returned to America when he was fifteen. German, then French, then English—this was the order of his linguistic evolution, to which Greek and Latin had been added quite early for, like Joyce,

*Eugene Jolas and James Joyce*

he was the object of especial attention on the part of the Catholic pedagogues, and he actually did spend two years in the Seminary in Metz. Being he himself convinced that he did not have the vocation to become a priest, he was taken out of the seminary at the age of fourteen and before he was sixteen, he left for America. There the direst, most sordid poverty and loneliness, plus a sense of violent revolt against both the Church and society drove him to the need for alcoholic oblivion, that he and Joyce shared till the end.

Fortunately, neither Joyce nor Jolas felt that "need for alcoholic oblivion" too frequently, for if so they would not have been able to function as brilliantly as each did in his own field. However, throughout his lifetime, Jolas was driven by an abhorrence of injustice as well as a desire to reshape the world. He never forgot the poverty he had suffered in Brooklyn where he first worked as a delivery boy in a grocery store, nor did he ever forget the cruelties he witnessed as a reporter for a Waterbury, Connecticut newspaper, covering some of the notorious Palmer raids.

His weapon for revolt—a natural one for a man with his linguistic background and his passion for language—was to be the word.

He began his literary career as a journalist, working for the Waterbury *Republican,* the New York *Daily News* and other American newspapers, including one in New Orleans. His eventual goal was to have a magazine of his own, through which to express his ideas and give expression to the ideas of others. While in New Orleans, he had seriously considered taking over a faltering small publication called *Double-Dealer,* but the idea was abandoned. It was not revived until several years later, when he was back in Europe, working as a reporter for the Paris *Tribune.*

Jolas and his statuesque and charming wife—the former Maria MacDonald from Kentucky—had followed the progress of Paris's little magazines with interest and enthusiasm. They were especially enthusiastic about *This Quarter* and deeply saddened to hear of the death of Ernest Walsh. On the day of Walsh's funeral they sent a telegram saying they would like to continue the tradition that Walsh had started, in publishing the best of the avant-garde writers.

Preparations for the magazine began, and the heavy-set, broad-shouldered, energetic man, with the fervent look in his eyes, sought out the finest writing for *transition*'s debut. Jolas's standards were high and his aims clear. The monthly magazine was subtitled "An International Quarterly for Creative Experiment," and it offered American writers "an opportunity to express themselves freely, to experiment . . . and to avail themselves of a ready, alert and critical audience." Jolas asked for a dialogue between the authors and that audience and hoped to create the climate for it in his magazine, which was to be "a proving ground for the new literature, a laboratory for poetic experiment." Jolas wrote: "It is the artist's search for magic in this strange world about us that I desire to encourage."

The first issue of *transition* was to appear in April 1927, and expectations for the magazine were high. The Jolases were among the best-loved figures in Paris's literary world. The poet Caresse Crosby characterized them as "grand, gifted people, with minds like new brooms, hearts like hearts." They were known, too, for their excellent taste as was the copublisher Elliot Paul. Robert Sage, expressing the hopes of the entire literary colony, wrote in the Paris *Tribune:*

With practically every American editor trapped in a blind-alley plugged by commercial interests, the advent of *transition* in Paris is of exceptional interest both to writers and to readers, for the program of his new literary magazine is joyfully devoid of gags and shackles. Circulation being a secondary matter, the artistic opinions of a business office are not required: being published in France, there is no risk of busybodies suppressing an issue because of an offending phrase. In short, there is no irrelevant machinery between the editor's desk and the linotype machine.

Elliot Paul and Eugene Jolas, who are responsible for *transition*, assume without rehearsal the role of creative editors. Both are alert to the manifestation of new influences and methods; both through their own writing have shouldered the problems that block the way to self-expression; the prejudices of each are visible only at the point where originality ends and bad writing begins. If the writer is articulate, they respect his full right to say what he wants about subjects of his own choosing.

The first issue of *transition* did not disappoint its readers. In it were contributions by the Americans Gertrude Stein, Kay Boyle, Hart Crane, Archibald MacLeish, and Ludwig Lewisohn. Among French writers were André Gide, Philippe Soupault and Robert Desnos, and Germany was represented by the work of Carl Sternheim. Jolas had gathered together in his magazine major figures from each of the three cultures that had shaped his own culture.

# TRANSITION

SUMMER NUMBER

## 30 Pages of

# JAMES JOYCE

## 35 - American Moderns - 35

## NEW YORK : 1928

WHAT FRENCH WRITERS
THINK OF AMERICA

# GERTRUDE STEIN

# ➤ ON SALE HERE

Most important of all, however, in that April 1927 issue of the new magazine was the contribution of James Joyce. The Irish writer had met Jolas through Sylvia Beach, at which meeting Joyce read aloud sections of his new book, *Work in Progress,* later to be titled *Finnegans Wake.* Jolas was enthralled by Joyce's daring and imaginative use of language and was eager to publish portions of the book in *transition.* This was the revolution he had been seeking, a revolution through words that could become a philosophy of life. He had written a manifesto that was called "The Revolution of the Word," and which began:

"Tired of the spectacle of short stories, novels, poems and plays still under the hegemony of the banal word, monotonous syntax, static psychology, descriptive naturalism, and desirous of crystallizing a viewpoint . . . we declare that the revolution in the English language is an accomplished fact." And the manifesto concluded with the militant words: "The plain reader be damned."

Joyce in his writing and bold experimentation was expressing Jolas's own thoughts, and the two became close friends. The Jolas household became a sanctuary for Joyce and his admirers, and the firm friendship between the Irish writer and Maria and Eugene Jolas continued until Joyce's death in 1941.

"The fact that an author's name is unknown will assure

his manuscript a more favorable examination," Jolas had stated, and *transition* published a large number of young and unknown writers. Jolas was a generous man and a tolerant one; he recognized talent even if its direction was different from his own. An excellent example is that of Matthew Josephson, who strongly opposed Joyce's work, finding it muddled and confused, but who was nonetheless published by *transition* and even appointed a contributing editor to the magazine by Jolas.

The list of important writers who contributed to *transition* is a long one. It includes, in addition to those already mentioned, Hemingway, cummings, Franz Kafka, and Vladimir Mayakovski—all of them appearing in the magazine before their names were known to a wide public. This little magazine, so large in influence, is a proud monument to the creativity of Paris in the twenties, an honest and bold experiment that succeeded and even, in its small way, caused a revolution.

# 12

# *There Are Too Few of Us*

It was these little magazines that drew a young and very gifted Canadian writer named Morley Callaghan to Paris in 1929, for it was in these magazines that his earliest short stories had been published. It was the magazines—*This Quarter* and *transition*—and it was Ernest Hemingway and Scott Fitzgerald.

Callaghan had been a law student in Toronto, and he had worked summers for the Toronto *Star*. There he met Hemingway, only five years his senior, but already a romantic figure as a European correspondent. Young Callaghan showed Hemingway the stories he had been writing, and the latter was enthusiastic; Hemingway showed Callaghan his own work, and the latter was even more enthusiastic.

The two men became friends; they talked about writers and writing and found vast areas of common interest. Hemingway talked of his life in Paris and how he missed it, and Callaghan decided that he, too, would go there someday.

When Hemingway, after the birth of his son, returned to the French capital, he spoke of Callaghan's stories to all those who might be influential in getting them published, and soon *transition* and *This Quarter* accepted stories by the hitherto-unknown Canadian. There followed a letter from the great New York editor, Maxwell Perkins, asking to see what Callaghan had written. Perkins was Hemingway's editor, and Callaghan was certain that Hemingway had been responsible for Perkins's interest. He learned that he was wrong, that Scott Fitzgerald, whom he had never met, had read his published stories and suggested that Perkins pursue the young writer. Scott Fitzgerald was young and rich and glamorous, the symbol of the Jazz Age, of good times and of success; and it was he who had made an effort to help a young writer he had never met.

Hemingway was in Paris as was Fitzgerald; so were the little magazines that had understood Callaghan's work. Nothing could stop the young Canadian from visiting the French capital, the capital of his literary world.

But there was one small warning of what was to come. Callaghan had written a story about a boxer—that was

*Ernest Hemingway in front of Shakespeare and Company*

Hemingway's field—and Hemingway was reported to have criticized Callaghan, saying the latter shouldn't write about things of which he was ignorant. However, Callaghan knew about boxing and had done a lot of it himself. This misunderstanding, he felt sure, could be easily cleared up. Morley Callaghan did not yet realize that literary friendships in Paris were fraught with rivalries and, unfortunately, often of short duration.

When the two men met in Paris, Hemingway put the young Canadian to the test at once. Taking out boxing gloves, he suggested that they spar. Before long, it was clear that the short dark Callaghan—who with his little moustache looked very much like a smaller version of Hemingway—had not been bluffing; he knew the sport and how to practice it. The two men, again friends, agreed that they would box together regularly at the American Club.

Now Callaghan wanted to meet his other benefactor, Scott Fitzgerald, and felt sure he could do so through Hemingway. The two American writers were reputed to be close friends, and it had been Fitzgerald, already an enormously successful writer with three novels to his credit, including *The Great Gatsby*, who had first spread the word of the young journalist's talent. When Fitzgerald spoke of Hemingway, they had not yet met, but when they did at a Paris café in 1925, they became good friends.

It was a strange friendship, between two opposites. In the early days the urbane, educated Fitzgerald had helped the rough-edged journalist, both by criticizing his work intelligently and by praising his stories in public. "There's magic in it," Fitzgerald told Gerald Murphy of *The Sun Also Rises*, and when he read *in our time* Fitzgerald re-

*F. Scott Fitzgerald with Zelda and Scottie*

marked that "Ernest's book is so much better than mine."

Fitzgerald admired Hemingway the man as much or more than he admired the writer. In many ways Hemingway was what Fitzgerald had wanted to be. The burly midwesterner was known for his skill as a boxer, a fisherman, and a skier; Fitzgerald had desperately tried to succeed as an athlete throughout high school and college, but he was small and basically unathletic, and his attempts to become a football hero were totally unsuccessful. Fitzgerald, too, wanted badly to be a war hero, but his division never got overseas during World War One, while the brave Hemingway had distinguished himself as an ambulance driver on the Italian front. In Fitzgerald's feelings toward Hemingway, there was an unmistakable element of hero worship. In spite of his own achievements, Scott Fitzgerald envied the sheer magnetic power and strength that distinguished Hemingway, who was the tough guy Fitzgerald wanted to be.

In time, Hemingway tired of Fitzgerald's effusive admiration and of the man himself. He complained that Fitzgerald's drinking made him irresponsible and that he didn't want the drunken writer arriving at his apartment at all hours of the day or night. In addition, he didn't at all like Zelda, Fitzgerald's fascinating but mentally ill wife. By 1929, when Hemingway learned that Fitzgerald was returning to Paris from the United States, he wrote to Perkins to say that he didn't want Fitzgerald to have his address.

Morley Callaghan knew none of this. He had had stars in his eyes when he came to Paris, and the stars for him were Hemingway and Fitzgerald. He was a gifted writer, but his importance during this period was his relationship to Fitzgerald and Hemingway. He badly wanted to be friendly with both of them, but each time he asked Hemingway about Fitzgerald, there was little or no response. Finally, he took matters into his own hands and dropped in, unannounced, to see Fitzgerald.

Scott and Zelda greeted him warmly, but as the visit went on it became clear that Zelda was in a nervous state and that Scott was drinking far too much. At one point Scott pulled out a copy of the manuscript of Hemingway's new novel, *A Farewell to Arms*, and read a portion of it to Callaghan. The latter was not impressed, and Fitzgerald was visibly annoyed. Suddenly he clumsily and unsuccessfully tried to stand on his head. "Would this impress you, Morley?" he asked.

Callaghan went away from that first meeting totally bewildered and confused. How could a brilliant and sensitive writer behave that way. And why, if they were no longer friends, did Fitzgerald have a copy of Hemingway's latest manuscript? The following day he told the story to Hemingway, but his response was merely a cold "Well, that's Scott."

That evening, when Callaghan and his wife returned to their apartment, they found three special delivery letters from Fitzgerald, each asking forgiveness for the unreasonable behavior. Shortly thereafter, the Fitzgeralds appeared, desperately apologetic. They had to be friends, Scott explained: "You see, Morley, there are too few of us."

Callaghan and Fitzgerald began to see a great deal of each other, but the Canadian remained puzzled about Fitzgerald's relationship to Hemingway. Fitzgerald kept asking questions about the author of *The Sun Also Rises,* first begging Callaghan to bring them together for dinner and then pleading with him to arrange for a meeting at one of their boxing matches. Though Callaghan continued to relay word of Fitzgerald to Hemingway, the latter didn't seem interested. Finally, exasperated, the puzzled Canadian told Scott that if he wanted to come along to watch a boxing session, he himself would have to ask Hemingway.

A week after this, as Callaghan was preparing to leave his home to pick up his sparring partner, there was a knock at the door. It was Hemingway and Fitzgerald, who had had lunch together and seemed on the best of terms. The surprised Callaghan was delighted: his two benefactors were friends again.

The three men arrived at the American Club and went right to the back room with the cement floor, which was usually used for gym exercises. While Hemingway and Callaghan got into their boxing trunks, Fitzgerald waited, happy to be a part of the match. He was to be timekeeper;

before the bout started, Hemingway carefully explained that each round was to be three minutes, with a minute in between.

The first round was uneventful; Fitzgerald watched the boxers intently, calling "time" at the end of three minutes, and then calling "time" again after the one-minute break. In the second round, however, things changed. Callaghan caught Hemingway on the mouth and the latter's lip began to bleed. Fitzgerald was horrified, and his face showed it. Was it possible that his hero was not invincible? Hemingway, too, seemed somewhat embarrassed in front of Fitzgerald, and his punches got wilder and more careless. Finally, it happened; he caught one of Callaghan's blows on the jaw and fell to the floor. Fitzgerald watched his hero sprawled out in front of him; then he looked at his watch. "Oh, my God," he shouted. "I let the round go four minutes."

Hemingway slowly arose and looked angrily at the terrified timekeeper. "All right, Scott," he said. "If you want to see me getting the shit knocked out of me, just say so. Only don't say you made a mistake." And he left the room.

Fitzgerald looked sick, and Callaghan was pained to see his tremendous suffering. He wondered what had really caused Hemingway's unnecessarily harsh words and what hidden resentment lay behind them. He assured the stricken

Fitzgerald that Hemingway himself would soon realize that if Fitzgerald had intentionally let the round go four minutes, he certainly would never have told anyone. Hemingway's words were merely those of a temporarily enraged man.

However, Fitzgerald could not be consoled. This day, to which he had so eagerly looked forward, had been ruined.

When Hemingway returned from the shower room where he had washed off the blood, he seemed calm, though he offered no retraction of his accusation. He and Callaghan resumed their sparring, after which the three writers went to have a drink at a Montparnasse café. On the surface all was friendly and polite, yet Fitzgerald remained hurt and bitter, unable to understand why this man he so admired and even looked up to harbored such hostile feelings toward him.

Neither Fitzgerald nor Hemingway mentioned the matter to Callaghan again. The latter liked both of these men, yet he brooded about Hemingway's numerous broken friendships. There was Ford Madox Ford, who had recognized Hemingway's talents in the beginning and given him work—and now Hemingway only spoke contemptuously of him. There was McAlmon, too: he had been the first to publish a book of Hemingway's, and now the latter spoke of him mockingly if at all. Sherwood Anderson had praised and encouraged Hemingway and was then made fun of by him in *The Torrents of Spring*. These are the names mentioned by Morley Callaghan in his excellent book of memoirs, *That Summer in Paris*, but there were others— Gertrude Stein, Ernest Walsh, and now Fitzgerald.

Callaghan, a newcomer to Paris, did not know just how many rivalries and broken friendships there had been in those hectic Paris years. Perhaps the reason was the very intensity of those years of growth and self-discovery; perhaps people who once needed each other no longer wanted to be tied to those needs. The record is a sad one: Pound against Stein, Stein against Hemingway, Hemingway against practically everyone, practically everyone against McAlmon, McAlmon against Fitzgerald; Igor Stravinsky turned his back on George Antheil and Antheil rejected Pound. . . .

Creative men were wasting their energies in petty quarrels; to paraphrase Scott Fitzgerald, there were too few of these creative men.

The final chapter in the story of that day at the American Club, when Fitzgerald let a round go four minutes and Hemingway accused him of doing so on purpose, is just another example of wasted energy.

Morley Callaghan was already back in Canada when he read a piece in the New York *Herald Tribune* that shocked him. A book columnist reported that Morley Callaghan had knocked out the great athlete Ernest Hemingway in one round in Paris.

Callaghan was upset; he knew how precious the legend of Hemingway the strong man was to Ernest, and he hurried to correct the story in a letter to the newspaper. "Last Saturday I saw the story of the singular encounter between Ernest Hemingway and me," he wrote.

It is a fine story and you can imagine how much I regret not deserving such a reputation, but this ought to be said.

Eight or nine times we went boxing last summer, trying to work up a sweat and an increased eagerness for a glass of beer afterwards. We never had an audience. Nor did I ever knock out Hemingway. Once we had a timekeeper. If there was any kind of a remarkable performance that afternoon the timekeeper deserves the applause. . . . I do wish you'd correct that story or I'll never be able to go to New York again for fear of being knocked out.

Realizing the repercussions that the story might have, Callaghan wrote to Maxwell Perkins, enclosing a copy of his letter to the *Tribune*. But before his denial could be printed in the newspaper, he received a *collect* cable, not from Hemingway, but from Scott Fitzgerald: HAVE SEEN STORY IN HERALD TRIBUNE. ERNEST AND I AWAIT YOUR CORRECTION.

Callaghan was furious; for the first time he felt real

anger toward one of the men he had so admired. If Fitzgerald and Hemingway had seen the story, why hadn't *they* corrected it? And why was it Fitzgerald who sent the cable, and sent it collect?

Soon the truth came out. Hemingway admitted that it was he who made Fitzgerald send the cable, much against the latter's wishes. He accepted the entire blame for it. All Callaghan's anger toward Fitzgerald, Hemingway said, should really be directed toward himself, Hemingway. Later came an apologetic letter from Scott Fitzgerald, saying that the "stupid and hasty" cable had been an injustice.

It was a meaningless, useless squabble among immensely talented men who had better and more positive things to do. Yet, somehow, it was a symbol of the end of the spirit that was Paris in the twenties.

# *Afterword*

The spirit of good feeling and camaraderie that had prevailed among Paris's expatriate colony for the most part
of a decade came to an end. Useless squabbles were a sign
of its deterioration, and they are easily explained. "We
began to find ourselves, more and more, getting on one
another's nerves," wrote Samuel Putnam, an editor and
translator who was a part of those Paris years. They had
been years of self-examination followed by self-discovery,
but as each artist or writer or musician grew, discovering
his or her individuality in the process, quarrels and differ-
ences inevitably developed, artistic as well as personal. The
common cause of creator versus society dissolved, and as
it did, so did the bond among the creators.

There were concrete changes as well, which sensitive observers began to note as early as the middle of the twenties. For Phil Sawyer, former art critic of the Chicago *Tribune,* Montparnasse had undergone such a transformation by 1925 that he was ready to go home. The quarter, for him, was no longer charming or picturesque, and living there was no longer inexpensive. The Dôme had once been frequented by a family of artists; by 1925 Sawyer saw it as "a sort of open air post-graduate school for tourists to study life."

The best place from which to study Life those last years of the decade opened on December 27, 1927. It was a café called the Coupole. Situated near the Dôme, it was neon-lighted and enormous, dwarfing the smaller neighboring cafés along the boulevard, and setting the mood for the changing Montparnasse. Its opening night was a major event. Fifteen hundred people attended and consumed fifteen hundred bottles of champagne, three thousand hard-boiled eggs, ten thousand little sandwiches, and eight hundred cakes. Everyone attended the opening: artists, writers, musicians, even actors and actresses like Josephine Baker, the American who was the sensation of the Paris music halls. By five in the morning the police had to be called in to send away the last guests. The Coupole, with its gigantic pillars decorated by Kisling and Léger, immediately became the symbol of a gaudier Montparnasse, one of new and brightly lighted stores and nightclubs. It served a thousand meals a day and was crowded at all hours. Tourists packed its huge terrace to stare at celebrities and found themselves staring at other tourists; buses, filled with visitors who had already glimpsed Shakespeare and Company, slowed down in front of the Coupole in order to give more tourists a chance to look at more tourists.

Having lost their privacy, their sense of a community, the artists and writers were fleeing Montparnasse. The quarter was no longer free and comfortable; it had become an attraction.

"By 1928 Paris had grown suffocating," Scott Fitzgerald wrote. "With each new shipment of Americans spewed up by the boom the quality fell off, until towards the end there was something sinister about the boatloads."

The boom that afforded so many curious Americans an opportunity to travel to Gay Paree ended abruptly in 1929. On October 23 of that year the Wall Street stock market crashed. Hundreds of thousands of Americans lost their life savings, and the economy of the entire country—followed by that of Europe—was badly shaken. The incomes on which Americans in Paris lived dwindled and then ceased altogether. Over a short period of time they went home to face the reality of their hardships and to try to earn a living.

The time for self-discovery had come to an end. Janet Flanner, correspondent for *The New Yorker*, reported an all-too-typical newspaper advertisement: "For Sale, Cheap, Nice Old Château, 1 Hr. from Paris; Original Boiserie, 6 New Baths; Owner Forced Return New York Wednesday; Must have Immediate Cash; Will Sacrifice."

Many sacrifices were made. There was an end to extravagance. No more fabulous, elegant parties. There were few, if any, gala concerts or commissions to daring composers to write new avant-garde works, no people who would subsidize money-losing magazines. They were more concerned with failing businesses or a declining stock market. Paris was, according to George Antheil, "beginning to die a little."

That death did not come suddenly, all at once, but two deaths at the end of the twenties have come to be symbolic of the end of a very special period. On August 19, 1929, Sergei Diaghilev, the man who had done so much to enliven and enrich Paris in the twenties, died, nearly penniless, in Venice. With his death there died, too, a certain glamour and an imaginative spirit in the arts. Nothing could replace the excitement of an opening of the Russian Ballet or the premiere of one of its new creations.

On December 10 of that year a thirty-one-year-old American committed suicide in New York, and his death, too, took on a special meaning. His name was Harry Crosby; he was rich, handsome, and intelligent. The son of great wealth, he was educated at Groton and Harvard and seemed destined for a successful career as a banker. But like so many Americans, he ran to Europe, in search of a way of life. Arriving there with his beautiful wife Caresse, he worked briefly for an American bank in Paris until he had had enough. Breaking all ties with his past, he devoted himself to poetry (as well as to a hedonistic kind of sun worship), entering the Paris literary scene as director of the Black Sun Press, which published rare works of literature in deluxe editions; he was also an occasional contributor to *transition*. Crosby differed from most of the expatriates because of his unusual wealth, but he was similar to them in his endless and often frantic search for a new meaning to life. His death, while on a visit to New York, was never fully explained. His body was found on a bed, his arm around a young woman with whom he had evidently made a suicide pact. His search had been meaningless, and he chose the time and place at which to end it. He had been a well-known figure among the Americans in Paris, and his death stunned them; for many it seemed to signal the end of their own quests for something special that they had hoped to find in Paris.

Crosby was a minor figure, though he was representative

of many. The major figures had, for the most part, left Paris by the early thirties. Hemingway moved on—to Cuba, for most of his life. Pound was in Italy, and Stravinsky traveled throughout the world, finally settling in California. George Antheil returned to America, and Robert McAlmon, feeling that Paris was finished, headed for Mexico. Sylvia Beach and her extraordinary bookshop saw hard times; the bookshop was barely rescued through the efforts of its loyal friends.

Gertrude Stein and James Joyce stayed on, but they had always spent more time in their studios, alone, than they had among the people of the quarter. The Jolases, too, remained in Paris, but *transition* suspended publication for two years starting in 1930 for lack of funds and because Eugene Jolas felt his magazine had fulfilled its purpose. "There is nothing," he wrote, "on the horizon just now to encourage any continuation of literary activity." The magazine was eventually revived, but only on a sporadic basis. The other little magazines disappeared.

In 1932 even Harold Stearns left Paris. The Paris *Tribune* reported sadly on February 2 of that year:

The last blow to Montparnasse is the departure of Harold Stearns. He went to California where the warm sun revives tired people. He was tired of the monotony of his role. Harold was a cerebral solitary who lived pleasantly in a passive world, and he used to sit at the Sélect and dream of old episodes. Once there was great promise, but there is something epic about great resignation. The latter is an enticing achievement, and Harold will always be remembered as a legendary figure, a good compensation. . . . The passing of Harold Stearns is pointed to as one more symptom of its end.

The end of the American expatriate experience in Paris was also a beginning. When the Americans returned home, they found that things were not as bad as they had remembered them—or perhaps they never had been. American art and literature were vigorous and developing. Enriched by their experiences in France, these Americans were all the more prepared to take pride in the creative development of their own country. Nostalgic at first, sentimental about the fruitful years they had spent abroad, they soon found that it was possible to work in the United States. The Paris years were important and would not be forgotten, but for many of those Americans Gertrude Stein's prophecy had been fulfilled:

America is a rich and well nourished home but not a place to work. Your parents' home is never a place to work it is a nice place to be brought up in. Later on there will be place enough to get away from home in the United States, it is a beginning, then there will be creators who live at home.

# Bibliography

Allen, Frederick Lewis. *Only Yesterday.* New York: Harper & Brothers, 1931.

Antheil, George. *Bad Boy of Music.* Garden City: Doubleday, 1945.

Bainbridge, John. *Another Way of Living.* New York: Holt, Rinehart and Winston, 1968.

Baker, Carlos. *Ernest Hemingway: A Life Story.* New York: Charles Scribner's Sons, 1969.

Balakian, Anna. *André Breton.* New York: Oxford University Press, 1971.

Beach, Sylvia. *Shakespeare and Company.* New York: Harcourt, Brace, 1959.

Bridgman, Richard. *Gertrude Stein in Pieces.* New York: Oxford University Press, 1970.

Brinnin, John Malcolm. *The Third Rose: Gertrude Stein and Her*

*World*. Boston: Little, Brown and Company, 1959.

Callaghan, Morley. *That Summer in Paris*. New York: Coward-McCann, 1963.

Charters, James ("The Barman") as told to Morrill Cody. *Hemingway's Paris*. New York: Tower Publications, 1965.

Cowley, Malcolm. *Exile's Return*. New York: The Viking Press, 1951.

————. *A Second Flowering*. New York: The Viking Press, 1973.

Crespelle, J.-P. *Montparnasse vivant*. Paris: Librarie Hachette, 1962.

Crosby, Caresse. *The Passionate Years*. Carbondale and Edwardsville: Southern Illinois University Press, 1968.

Ellmann, Richard. *James Joyce*. New York: Oxford University Press, 1959.

Flanner, Janet. *An American in Paris*. New York: Simon and Schuster, 1940.

————. *Paris Was Yesterday*. New York: The Viking Press, 1972.

Ford, Hugh (ed.). *The Left Bank Revisited: Selections from the Paris* Tribune *1917–1934*. University Park: The Pennsylvania State University Press, 1972.

Glassco, John. *Memoirs of Montparnasse*. Toronto, New York: Oxford University Press, 1970.

Hemingway, Ernest. *A Moveable Feast*. New York: Charles Scribner's Sons, 1964.

Joost, Nicholas. *Ernest Hemingway and the Little Magazines: the Paris Years*. Barre, Mass. Barre Publishers, 1968.

Josephson, Matthew. *Life Among the Surrealists*. New York: Holt, Rinehart and Winston, 1962.

Loeb, Harold. *The Way It Was.* New York: Criterion Books, 1959.

McAlmon, Robert. *Being Geniuses Together: 1920–1930.* Revised and with supplementary chapters by Kay Boyle. London: Michael Joseph, 1970.

Milford, Nancy. *Zelda.* New York: Harper & Row, 1970.

Mizener, Arthur. *The Far Side of Paradise: A Biography of F. Scott Fitzgerald.* Boston: Houghton Mifflin, 1965.

————. *The Saddest Story: A Biography of Ford Madox Ford.* London: The Bodley Head, 1971.

Norman, Charles. *Ezra Pound.* New York: Macmillan, 1960.

————. *The Magic-Maker: E. E. Cummings.* New York: Macmillan, 1958.

Paul, Elliot. *The Last Time I Saw Paris.* New York: Random House, 1942.

Penrose, Roland. *Picasso: His Life and Work.* New York: Harper & Brothers, 1958.

Putnam, Samuel. *Paris Was Our Mistress: Memoirs of a Lost and Found Generation.* New York: The Viking Press, 1947.

Reid, B. L. *The Man from New York: John Quinn and His Friends.* New York: Oxford University Press, 1968.

Siohan, Robert. *Stravinsky.* London: Calder and Boyars, 1965.

Steegmuller, Francis. *Cocteau.* Boston: Little, Brown, 1970.

Stein, Gertrude. *Paris France.* New York: Liveright, 1970.

Stock, Noel. *The Life of Ezra Pound.* London: Routledge & Kegan Paul, 1970.

Stravinsky, Igor. *An Autobiography.* New York: Simon and Schuster, 1936.

Thomson, Virgil. *Virgil Thomson*. New York: Alfred A. Knopf, 1966.

Tomkins, Calvin. *Living Well Is the Best Revenge*. New York: The Viking Press, 1971.

Turnbull, Andrew (ed.). *The Letters of F. Scott Fitzgerald*. New York: Charles Scribner's Sons, 1963.

————. *Scott Fitzgerald*. New York: Charles Scribner's Sons, 1962.

Unterecker, John. *Voyager: A Life of Hart Crane*. New York: Doubleday and Company, 1970.

White, William (ed.). *By-line: Ernest Hemingway*. New York: Charles Scribner's Sons, 1967.

Wickes, George. *Americans in Paris: 1903–1939*. New York: Paris Review Editions, Doubleday and Company, 1969.

Wilenski, R. H. *Modern French Painters*. New York: Vintage Books, 1960.

# Photocredits

*The author wishes to acknowledge for use of photographs:*
Culver Pictures: 14, 92, 147
Dance Collection, The New York Public Library at Lincoln Center; Astor, Lenox and Tilden Foundations: 97
Hamilton College: 132
Music Division, The New York Public Library at Lincoln Center; Astor, Lenox and Tilden Foundations: 16, 90, 95
The New York Public Library Picture Collection: Frontispiece, xiv, 3, 5, 7, 12, 47, 50, 112, 120, 136
Pictorial Parade: 44
Princeton University, The Sylvia Beach Collection: 22, 27, 28, 32, 38, 39, 56, 65, 67, 69, 71, 73, 76, 78, 83–86, 102, 106, 118, 125, 134, 140
Yale University, The Beinecke Rare Book and Manuscript Library, Collection of American Literature: 18, 41, 104, 145

# *Index*